To Samantha
with love
30/03/2016

Heal Your Heart

by
Anthony Omogbehin

authorHOUSE®

AuthorHouse™ UK Ltd.
500 Avebury Boulevard
Central Milton Keynes, MK9 2BE
www.authorhouse.co.uk
Phone: 08001974150

First published by AuthorHouse 1/25/2010

ISBN: 978-1-4490-2608-0 (e)
ISBN: 978-1-4343-5052-7 (sc)
ISBN: 978-1-4343-5053-4 (hc)

Printed in the United States of America
Bloomington, Indiana

This book is printed on acid-free paper.

This book is dedicated to my dearly beloved daughters Jasmine Similolu and Mayomi Shirley Omogbehin. They are the sunshine that light up my window in the winter that life is.

Also, to the memory of my late mum Christiana Olufunmilayo Omogbehin, an astute, beautiful, extremely quiet and unassuming lady who let her good deeds speak for her. She was cruelly snatched away by what I now realise to be cancer of the liver at a tender age of just 38 years.

Main

Book 1
The Love That Could
Have Healed Your Heart

My Stupid Heart

I am finally back in my beloved city
Then I found out there was something missing!
I looked everywhere for it
And yet I couldn't find it
Then it suddenly dawned on me,
My broken heart had refused to come with me
It had decided instead to remain

It has decided to wait at the side of the beautiful one
The cute one
The intelligent one
The jewel of the great country
The daughter of 'the most beautiful city in the world'
That is the one who has my heart

How stupid you are I say to my heart
Don't you ever learn?
Don't you ever remember?
Don't you know how sore you are?
Don't you realise you need to mend?

But my heart was far away
My heart would never listen to a word I say

The damsels of the home country are calling loud
They are calling out to my heart
'Come home with us' they say
'We are beautiful
We are elegant
We are the greatest lovers
What we lack in confidence we make for in charm
We love you
We want you
Come home with us' again they say.

Alas my stupid heart will not listen
My heart will never learn
Yet again it had left me alone
It has developed a mind of its own
It has made home at the side of the jewel
It has grown those wings yet again
It is ready to perch.

Again I call out to my heart
Please come back to me I plead
Don't you realise you belong here?
Don't you realise the jewel is not ours?
Don't you realise it is already taken?
Don't you understand it'll never be released?
Don't you realise it'll never be free?

I think I know what is wrong with you my heart
My heart craves pain
My heart loves sorrow
My heart wants to be damaged

Who will save my stupid heart?

Would She Let Me Stroke Her Hair?

I know the moment that I fell for her
It happened so suddenly but not by chance
We met as we were supposed to be
To form a bond that's meant for life
By fate my heart was given
Instinctively but to last for life

It was just a hug that pulled the plug
A kiss below the chin
A cuddle to say so long
To one who is hurt and aching all around
An accident event that never was planned
An embrace from the heart
In the burning scorching sun
In a room that was meant for work
A gentle collision of chests
But then our hearts were met
Entangled in a web of love

I never thought this was real
Because I thought I was still in one
I thought the rule was true for all
You couldn't be in love so soon
Not when you've just been dashed
Not when hurt and in deep despair

But that rule did not apply
It did in times gone by
For people that lived awhile
The new don't follow a guide
These new hearts respect no one
They go where they wish at will
Without a hint of fear
Of the danger along the way

That indeed has been the case with mine
It gave itself without my wish
Pleading I made to no avail
It still remained the place it'd found

Everyday passes and it's still the same
It suddenly came to me
Without a notice of what's to come
Delivering the news of what it'd found
That it wasn't a dream at all
That I'd better accept my lot
That it'd found a cute young one

It could be a place I will find my rest
A place of joy and hope
A place of excitement and ecstasy
A place of fun and fantasy
A place to chill and mill
Solid and sure and real
A virgin land that seeks a man
An explorer to reveal its truths

How I have suddenly found myself engulfed
Without a doubt at all in love
With this fair angel that's caught my heart
Now I'll detail what I mean

This smart lady of mine is neat
Everything she wears to match
Necklace, wristwatch and even rings
All match the colour chosen for the day
Clever in every respect
Determined to make her mark
But stepping on no one's toes
She's humble to a fault

Respectful of young and old
She greets all on the street
Tramps and rich alike

Tall and straight she is
With legs long and shapely
Stretching as far as her ears
Elegant in her poise and gait
She walks not like a girl
But not even like a boy
As fast as gazelle in the savannah
On her toes the pressure is felt
Leaning forward with chests out turned
Exposing cute long arms

Beautiful to behold
Lovely to be with
Reliable in all her ways
As calm and reassuring as anyone
You can count on her in everyway
Disappointment, no, that's not a word

No errand is too mean for her
No job is too humble to take
No assignment is too far to attain
Ambitious as a man would be
But with malice she won't be found

White she likes in shirts
Black she prefers in pants
But turquoise is more like her
To suit her auburn hair
Crisp and wispy and straight
Blowing gently in the wind
Well below the shoulders they rest
Like stalks of barley and wheat
At mid summer and harvest time

At the twilight of the day
Browned by the scorch of the sun
As that great one sets in the west
They are even cute, sweet and smart
When tied in a ponytail
The strands of copper in them
Very visible for all to see
Revealed is a narrow cute face
That lights up with a smile

Let me tell you more about this smile
She smiles with the entire body
Her face and cheeks reveal two lovely dimples
With an expression that says 'I am here to stay
And very glad you've come my way'

And silvery blue eyes to match
Which seem to have seen a lot
Pain and joy and hope alike
They open as wide as a saucer
Flying in the skies above
They open wide and big I said
Whenever excited or irritated
The former is mostly the case

Her body is full of hair
Not even her arms are spared
She hardly shows her legs
Of those we cannot say
Golden for every strand
In sharp contrast with her ginger head
I wonder where else these can be found
Along with the beauty spots
And freckles brown like chocolate
These seem to be everywhere

A voice like that of a bird
With a slick Saxonian pitch
The tongue of Gauls of old
Spoken in the sweetest of ways
Delightful to the drums
Exciting to the loins
To light the fire of the mind

She's got a behind that says I'm here
Look at me if you wish
Deal with it if you can
I'm pretty and I'm proud of it
They have a life of theirs
Responding to hip and hop
As the owner moves along

How I'd love to rub her back
Massaging its every curve
With oils expensive and rare
Filling all the crevices and gaps
Releasing the pleasure from within the being
Electric shocks that grab the brain
Waves that travel everywhere

Could I put these hands of mine
Gently around her chest
That slim tall torso of hers
Embedded in a firm curvaceous frame
Preferred by everyman
Then her breasts will heave and sigh
Her heart will beat like a drum
Pounding along to the beat of the konga
Faster and faster it will go
Until love takes effect
Releasing all the stress

I keep asking myself
Would she let me stroke her hair?
Rubbing my hands gently through the strands
Back and forth, to and fro
As they blow in response to the breeze
Under the apple tree
I'll pick each strain a time
My index doing the job
Drawing patterns unique and pure
Provoking pleasure from deep inside

Will I ever be made to touch?
Her slender waste that's shaped like the moon
Will I ever hug her so?
Our breasts touching as they did before
Will I ever make her scream?
Will she ever yet behold?
This feminine body God gave to me
That few have yet beheld

Whenever she draws near to me
I behold the beauty that's her breasts
Then to teeth that's white and set
In jaws you want to hold so tenderly

I stop to think when she's about
A look from her and I start to shake
I look at her and I feel my pulse
Racing as in a sprint
My brain feels as if it's dead
My heart starts to beat like mad
Pumping fire through my veins
My loins swelling to the brim

Drips of sweat all over my skin
Juices streaming from down below
My voice shaking as if I'm drunk

Legs vibrating of their own accord
Just as if they've had a shock

I want to hold her yet I fear
I want to hug her yet I can't
I want to kiss her but then I freeze
I want to touch her but then I lose my mind
To kiss her back till it aches and explodes
Sending electric through her brain

I say to myself there will come a day
A day to express the love I feel
To touch her lips and nose
Then kiss them gently and yet tenderly so
The back end of her small white teeth
Our tongues locked as one and tight
Like boxers clinched in the boxing ring
Or like twins born on the island of Siam

Gently and gently and gently at first
Then slowly and slowly increasing the pace
Then maybe roughly as time goes by
Faster and faster and faster
Exactly as indeed she wants it to be

Maybe she would let me stroke her hair
Kissing her on the chin as she longs to be
In a bear hug gentle and kind
Those butts that long for a caress
Those beautiful bottoms that delight the soul
My right hand travelling through the crack between
To squeeze and hold them tight
The proper way I mean
So that they take another life
To reach the heights they are meant

What about those eyes of hers
They tell a lot more than she says
The truth they tell with no pretence
They say she surely feels the same
She wants to be touched but cannot ask
To have her hair stroked like no one has
Making her feel like the queen she is
Taking her where she's never been
I pray for once she says okay
Never again would she want to go

But wait I say to you
This light companion of mine
Of northern birth and clime
She longs for these things indeed
But afraid she is of things unknown
She's been with one for years
She's sure as hell it is safe
But the doubts have now surfaced
In leaps and bounds they have come

What on earth will the people say?
To learn she'd left with a man
A man of southern birth
With skin as dark as charcoal

Could she ever take the plunge?
In the deep and dark world that's there
A world of fun and joy
A land of make belief
Where dreams come out true

Maybe for once she'll lose her guard
To taste the fun she craves
A word of it she'll never say

Will she accept to go with him?
For a night that makes dreams real
To have the inside of her legs caressed
By kisses that are sent by God
The reverse side of her thy
The tip of her slender toes
Till she lies wasted on the bed
Staring at the twinkling stars
In paradise itself they'll be
Making love until day dawn breaks

Epilogue

When I look into my future
I see a fair blue blonde
Or is it really auburn or ginger for that matter?
But I never loved blondes before
I hate their fair pale skin
The dark always had my heart
Even if it's just their hair
What is wrong with me and my heart?
Could it be something about her?
Could it in fact be her that I saw?
I just hope it's not a dream

If things ever go wrong
If it doesn't work
And tried your best you did
Conscience as clear as snow
If it makes you sad
When your heart needs a walk
When your soul needs a rest
Remember I'll still be there
Waiting in the wings for you
Patiently for your call
To have you in my arms
Stroking your hair like I said I would
This time to eternity

But Then I Saw You Smile

It was a cold dreary spring day
In a land very far away
To which we'd come in search of the sun and a tan
By the sea that's called 'the pond'
Great and mighty today as it's been for ages

The desert astride but not at bay
Threatening to engulf all what remains of the land
The shrubs and the dates are evidence of this
The flowers of which betray the truth
In splendid colours they adorn the land
Creeping around whatever piece of soil they could find

There we waited for the bus back home
In this town that suits its name
Those bendy buses like the ones at home
Our home ruled by a man who never conforms
Where the queen lives who never really laughs
Yet none can claim they don't do their jobs
With two friends of mine we waited in vain
For this snake of a machine that just wouldn't arrive
Then at last it stopped by us
Everyone rushed to find a place on board

It was first your charm that caught my eye
You and your friend with both hands locked
Then a glance behind that says 'we're here'

Immediately I thought I'd stay near you
Told my friends I'll go for this
These maidens of the land could be worth the while

Then arrived this woman and her mate
Her man you could tell by the rings they wore
Complaining she did that she'd lost her phone
In a tongue they speak in Paris of the sky
She laid the blame at the door of your land

Then it was your charm became a frown
You won't accept your land to be besmirched
You said her plight was common to all lands
That you could lose you prize in any clime
That north or south there are thieves within
Even in the east far way rogues abound
More so the west where it's as common as day

Then it was your frown began to lift
Gradually your face was clear to see
And what a spectacle indeed I beheld!
A Phoenician face like those ancient Roman paintings
Ones I read and watched when I was a child
Eyes as wide and clear as glass itself
As beautiful as the sun in the middle of the day

In sockets so fine as if they're carved
Lashes straight and glowing like ebony
I'll never forget the deep brown of them
Your trident hair tied back in the finest wrap

I mean I'd never seen eyes like yours in my life
And those lips that pout and pause
How very soft they appear to be
How much softer they'd feel on mine
Is it your cheekbones that defy the mind?
How very set indeed they are
Housing your mouth which I'm sure cannot be bought
Not even with all the money in the world

Then suddenly you broke into a smile
What was it that teased you so?
Was it the joke from your friend by me?
Or the constant tease and jibe from that old mate
How very pretty the sight I saw?

A set of teeth that's white like snow
On gums so pink they glow in the sun
Each tooth had a place of its own
Verses can be written of those alone
This smile lit the beauty of your face
It seemed to me it even brightened the bus
Because suddenly all on it were laughing with you
You bring the sun with you wherever you go

Then suddenly my stone heart began to melt
Even then I had not beheld
The spectacle that'll follow this smile of yours
Because that woman spoke the tongue again
The tongue they speak in Tuscany by the sea
She began to sob and cry aloud
All her face red and wet
Dripped with tears that flowed from her broken heart

Then it was I saw another bit of you
Your heart went out to her at once
To this woman who had dared to demean your land
You reached out as if to give her a cuddle
Your eyes sorry and complete in compassion

You thought over what you could do to help
But nothing could be done to soothe her pain
Not even words of consolation
Sweetly translated to her mother tongue
It was just a trigger I thought for this woman
A volcanic release for the pain that lay in for years
This woman had been sad for ages I thought

Only the loss of a phone it took to release the torrent
A dam that'd been itching to burst for hey
To release the pain that she'd held within for so long
In the deepest recesses of her heart.

Then it was my attention returned to you
You'd told me twice about yourself
Giving your name that I never could catch
Then for a third time I asked again
But you'd made up your mind never to tell
All my pleading was yet in vain

Did you resist me because of your friends?
Or was it the fact I wasn't paying attention
Was it the fear of man that held you back?
You said you've been betrothed to another one
To none of my pleading will you respond
I made an appointment to see you again
Pleading my innocence the zillionth time

Will I ever see your lovely face again?
Your wonderful pale skin
Finer even than the golden sands of the Sahara
Your deep brown eyes
Shinier than the polished surface of the desert rose
Will you let me show you that endless love like the desert road?
Or will I forever be consoled by the relief on the wall
Of those Phoenician women of ancient times
Mothers of the great Carthaginians that ruled the seas
Them who gave the Romans a run for their money

Will I ever be able to ask?
Will I ever be able to speak?
To speak the truth about my life
That God has indeed blessed me with everything
It's him I call to be my witness today
That these feelings for you are true and sure

The Almighty is a witness that I love you so
May Allah be the judge if I tell a lie
May Allah be praised if indeed it's true
That what you said to me indeed was a fact
That you are committed to someone
And indeed couldn't ever be free

If in truth this wasn't the case
Right on my knees I beg in appeal
I must request you to be my wife
To provide the peace I crave at home
My companion for life and forever more
To be my bride in a land that's great
And continues to be great without producing a thing

Please be mine and I'll be yours
I promise to be faithful and chaste for life
I'll give anything for this to be true
For in you I have met my partner for life.

A lady in central Souse, Tunisia

Permit You Must

I saw your face and thought you are cute
That the beauty of you is second to none
And then you smile and lit the hall
Dimples on cheeks delicate and fine
Your well set teeth were a delight to seek

Then you spoke with a voice from up above
Words that show you are clever and bright
Your grey blue eyes glowing in the light
A place fair skin with no defects at all
Hair well combed to the shoulder their length

Your countenance was peaceful and calmed the crowd
You told of the love you felt for mum
How much you'll give her as time permits
How happy she was to have a 'baby' like you
Generous and kind and willing to give her all
To make a difference to the life of all your own

That is why any man would be drawn to you
Young or old middle or mate
But how many men would see your charm
When it lays buried in the shadow that's cast
How many men would see your smile?
The way you smiled on the bus ride home
When you won't accept the beauty of you
Consoling yourself that your beauty lays deep within
I look like mum you say to all
Look at her and nothing can be done
Will you ever permit yourself the fame that's yours?
To let the world see you the way you are

What a night indeed you would have had?
In the arms of someone attractive and strong
But most of all attracted to you
Like magnet to steel he is glued to you
Seeing in you the good that you promise
A beautiful girl with nothing to lose
But endowed you are with a million stars
Your future is bright and your life will be good

Only if with someone who can bring the very best of you
Despite our age the affinity is sure
The chemistry between is a delight to behold
You can't deny how hard it was to be peeled away
Especially as we rode along on that house of steel
The coach that runs without a horse

The beach was waiting for us to walk
Moonlight that you would have seen like never before
The stars of heaven would have lit our path
As we strode along side by side
On the golden sands of the Med itself

But then you stopped still in your tracks
Denying yourself the pleasure that lay within
A craving you've had the whole night long
Stopped yourself as you've clearly done before
Hiding again in the shadow of the one you love
Your mum she is and a good one too
But would you ever permit yourself a chance to live
Pulling away from the shadow, the image she casts.

Book Ii
Those Cities That
Inspire The Soul

'The Most Beautiful City in the Weld'

What a place you've proved to be?
I'll shout aloud your praise to all
A place to rest and a place of hope
The peace you bring to all within
To live and love within your gates

Your rivers flow from deep within
Also without is where they are
They keep you green in all your ways
From year to year they never cease
They flow like showers from up above
Is it the lake that keeps you so?
A lake that was dug by a man of old
Or is it the rain that never stops

Woods abound within your walls
For all to go and find some peace
Some go to snug and kiss at night
The fear of harm does not arise
Even the stars from heavens above
Cannot but marvel at the sight of you
Your beauty is clear for all to see

Let me tell some more about what I find
The wonders I found since I came to you
You're like the sun in the skies above
Surrounded by stars as pretty as you
Your county lanes are a marvel indeed
They are just as precious as you yourself
You are so green and keen to please
The horses graze in your grass all day
Their hoofs attached to your gentle ground

The whole world has come to you
To behold the spectacle of men at play
Kicking the round ball that earns them loads
But then they are amazed at your beauty and brim
They cannot but wonder at the way you've turned
From disaster you've risen and now you're great
As great as any of the towns I've seen
In fact much greater than some of the greats I've been

Your girls have come from every home
The roofs of which are red as blood
They come with buttons as bare as bell
Their faces fair and glow like snow
The snow that dwells on the slopes above
These hills abound in lands below
Atop the Alps of Bavaria and more

Back to the maidens that dwell in you
They show a joy that's deep within
Their bottoms rolling as if they're wheels
With deep green eyes like emerald itself
Some as blue as the deep monstrous sea
I cannot but marvel at the gait of these
Giants they are in their own rights
There is one of them that's caught my eye
I know for sure she won't be mine

Your men are big and strong for sure
They are not exempt from praise at all
Taller that most I have seen alive
They are just as fair as the dames in you
They greet on the streets all that they meet
To offer a hand to those in need
All the time with a smile in tow

They do amaze at the sight they bring
Determined they are to achieve their best
Even at that they'll never rest
Their quest is ever for make belief
Perfect they imagine themselves to be
But that is left for the world to judge

You have a zoo that is second to none
The animals friendly as if they are pets
Big and small they flock to men
They get a pat for their friendly smile.

Your roads are broad and safe to thread
Your trains are as clean as they are prompt
You promise a place that's good for all
The peoples abound as proof of this
Are they really as happy as they do appear?
They eat the meals as made at home
At ease they feel in your boulevard

Can anyone dispute your claim to fame?
To be the best at everything
The jewel of the north they say you are
Of this indeed my doubt is nil

The Town Hall (Reicht Haus) in Hannover, Germany. What you won't see in this picture are the splendid parks that surround this impressive building and a few yards away is the Marschee an artificial lake built during the Second World War. It has the biggest pikes I have ever seen and teems with many other kinds of fish

Tinsel City

Oh my dearly beloved city
What on earth could compare to you?
You who sit at the centre of the world
You who dictate the time for all mankind
You to whom the world looks for direction
You who have become a model for great and small
What could be said about you not yet said?
How could one ever describe you and get it right?

Is it the fact you were born a long time ago
Even the Romans met you here
Is it the fact you sit within an Island
Small it is but feared in everywhere
Is it the river that flows within your midst?
So famous that even a juvenile whale found its fame

Is it the numerous parks that adorn your precincts?
None in the world boast of as many or as distinct
At least none other has the prefix 'Royal'
One couldn't even remember the number of them
Thirty three, sixty six or ninety nine

One of these is really special indeed
It's a park that one could Hyde
Away from the sorrows that invade your life
It's a place you can bewail your grief
Without a fear you'd be set upon
This very park indeed has been great to me
In my hardest of times it was a comfort home
Where my sorrows and pains were drowned
In a fountain dug in honour of a queen,
A queen of hearts that could have been but never was

Even your buses are unique to you
They are double decked and elegant to watch
Some of them bend like the anaconda
Red like blood the colour of them
No other towns have what you have
Taxis that look like the coaches of old
Rode by the nobles, the royals and their families

Then there's that family that live in the Buck
Or in that castle that's swept by the Wind
How their ship continues to sail
How many times we thought they'll sink
No great harm done seems to affect their fame
Now they've got two boys that love to dance
How very splendid the places they live
All over town the spread of these

Peoples of all nations assemble in you
Complete with their bags strapped to their backs
In you they found a home for all
All the tongues of the world they speak in you
All their meals are cooked in you
How many palates find their delight?
In those glowing corners they call their home

How much more I could say about you?
How very narrow your streets have been?
But then elegantly kept over myriads of years
Isn't that why the nations have flocked to you?
To see your fame and feed your birds
That square of yours busy as a beehive
But then you say it's not enough
You continue to build and build for more

Your iron tracks are the longest in the world
As under the ground they wind along
They form a network that is second to none

How very envious the world views your fame
Especially as you keep remaking yourself
Ever positioning yourself at the centre of fun

You've even built an eye that is taller than most
It's come to rest on the river of Thames
And that tower they used to execute
Where the men in red still protect
Even there the sightseers go
Especially the men and women of Japan
Arigato! Arigato! Yorushko! they greet
All the while clicking away on their small machines
Never for ones bothering to pause or look

You have the gardens that are planted by men
Of this was a man that refused to Kew
To the west of town he built his name

You are a city that refuses to sleep
Not even at night as is common to men
But danger lurks if you choose to mess
Around the corner in the middle of the night

Your stadiums are full of men of sorts
Most of them pregnant from beer
Even then it's not enough
Because you've won the race to host
The run by men the crème of the world
Another incentive for you to build
Despite the recent one you built with rings
How can anyone ever match up to you?
When your appetite for building will not relent

Your shops are full in every way
Big in town and massive without
The corner shops I'm pleased to say
Are now owned and run by the men of the Indies

Only on the Ox ford they haven't found a way
This street of yours has a daily 'million man march'
With crowds spending their monies as if its sand
With the Russians at the head of the line
Their Rubbles now worth its while in gold
Thanks to the goodwill of Mr Gorbachev
With his *perestroika* and *glasnost*.

There's a place where dummies are beheld
With a name that frenchies bear
I can't believe the sight of this
People wait like ants to pay their way
To see these images of every kind
Effigies of men living as well as dead
Patiently they stand just to catch a glimpse

Your obsession with history is clear to all
Accurate records you've kept for decades and more
Isn't that why I love you so?
You are a bridge for me connecting to the past
I share my feelings with millions of men
We flock to you in hordes of hope
To a city comparable with none in the world

Could I possibly say enough about you?
In you have lived the men of fame
The blue stones on walls are evidence of this
In fact a king that changed the world
He wanted a fresh flame to replace his old love
And won't take a word from the Latin priest
There's also that man of letters and verses
In the south of Kent he lived and died
And the man of science that threw the apple down
There are lots more I couldn't name at once
They lived and died within your walls
One of these is the one that shakes the spear
What great lines he wrote for all.

Before I knew you I'd heard of you
From childhood my dream were all about you
I even told tales about being in you
The dreams I beheld in the middle of the night
Of cabs driven by men and women alike
One old man believed these wishes of mine
And took to heart the words I said
Never for once doubting the veracity of them
Never thinking they were conjectures of the heart
I've never done such a thing in life
Telling tales to grease the bright

Very likely its true of many like me
It took them dreaming to realise their worth
Millions more fulfil their wish in life
They've come to you and have made their mark.

But how very quickly you are changing 'my love'
Everyone thinks you are reaching your peak
That at this moment there is none your kind
Not even the city with the tower of steel
Nor the city of hearts that's lost its soul
Don't even talk about that city of angels
This is now full of vice

But my piercing eyes have looked you through
I can see for sure that you rot from within
Your values are dying and your virtues disappearing
It's partly the fault of that arrogant and bossy bunch
The press for grains they call themselves
Obsessed they are with nakedness and obscenity
Destruction they bring to everything on their way
Promoting mediocrity instead of excellence
Dictating opinions like Stalin and Mussolini
When in fact their job is to report the news

They build and destroy with the stroke of their pen
Making heroes of delinquent youths
Kids who are now destroying the wealth of our clan
But there was one who defied this norm
It's that famous soccer player of cockney climes
He refused the destiny you dictated for him
It's that guy married to the pencil thin wife
That is ever so shy as she faces the flash
The guy who went to the loo to score a goal

At first you courted him like a beautiful bride
Then you worshipped him like a god from on high
Then you turned on him like that feral beast
The one with seven heads in the Apocalypse
You wanted to devour him flesh and all
But he won't stay down this clever alek
A 'coup de grace' he pulled without a doubt
Now he's been called into the Galaxy
And as sure as hell you are back again
Leaking the crack of his polished bum

He may have been born working class
But defying the odds he's going to be a knight
And nothing you do can dissuade this destiny of his

Back to you again
You whose role is conscience of the people
But who have since forgotten your calling
See yourself celebrating mediocrity
Shame on you for worshipping ignorance
Because of you our streets are now unsafe
Kids killing kids for nothing but fun
They started out smashing the boxes to phone
Puking on the street as they returned from the pub
Cursing and shouting and without respect
But then you regard them as kings of the street .

These horrible celebrities behaving badly
They make us sick the sight of them
Spread eagled as they are in the centre of your papers
And those ones who kick the round object
They curse and kick on the field of play
But you lack the guts to speak against them
Because decadent as them you are in your private life
Shame on the custodians that've forgotten their place

See what you've done
Our taverns used to be centres of social contact
Where minds are rubbed and thoughts are born
Now our boys drink as if they're fish
And the girls compete with them in slush
Most give birth even before they are weaned
Their figures are now eleven rather than eight
They fool themselves claiming they're hour glass
Very soon we'd need more livers than gas
Who'd save us from this dire destiny of ours?
Who'll build the gyms that'll keep us fit?
Who'll save our kids from self destruct?

Now my city it's back to you
You claim to be a place for all don't you?
Then why on earth are all your bosses fair?
Even those ones that are supposed to fight the fire
With ceilings of glass you've build your works
Blocking access to those that are black and brown

Why is there so much separation within your midst?
Why do the Poles live on the western front?
Why do the Bengalis live in the deprived east?
Why do your police admit they are bad in loads?
Even then very slow to reform their ways

Why do you live in the past till now?
Closing the door to children of the poor
Why has misery never left your midst?
Why do myriads still sleep on the street?
And not that you have a weather that's kind to them
Why are your streets full of the excrement of dogs?
Why aren't they clean like the streets of the Gaul?

You cannot ever be truly great
Look over your shoulder my dear famous one
Unless you notice the threats from without
You'll never attain your potential to the full
Tapping up all the opportunities within
See the horizon and witness the threat
The locusts are coming and indeed are here
They've come by train the Orient express
Only travelling in the direction of the west
Millions of them to decimate the land
Not like the brown ants you' had before
One of whom I confess I do belong
These locusts are bent on gorging the crops
They are proud and strong and enormous in size
With no respect for any at home
They'll trample on customs and laws alike
One of these locusts looked in the guard of the vault
Returning quickly to as safe haven in Mars
Bearing death dealing pollen as far as the grove
Creating a poor widow along his trail
A sweet young lady dignified, loyal and calm
Her only crime was her love for a honest man
Who dared to bare his man by speaking the truth

But should you fail to learn from Berlin
You will self destruct like Rome of old
May God Almighty never permit us such a fate

The London Eye. A marvel of engineering genius that makes Big Ben and the houses of parliament in in the background look and feel like little midgets

Celle

There is a town in north central Germany
That seems to stands tall above the rest
Not because of the size of her buildings
Not because she sits on a hill
There's probably one or two like her around
In this great country obsessed with greens
A nation that seeks to be perfect in everything
Of all that is done by man that is
For this great land I have respect
For it also a love is formed
Affection that's hard to describe in words
But there's one great town that's greater than all
Different in both my ears and my mind
My head swells as if it'll burst
Goose pimples spread all across my skin
As I behold the beauty that's beyond compare
I saw for once a sight of dreams
Of harmony between man and beasts
And tears of joy well up in my eyes.

What I saw was beyond compare
How man can work without destroying his home
Still retaining the beauties of nature that surround us so
The creations of God in Celle have found a home
No wonder it is they're not moving an inch
In its great pond rivers and streams
Fishes of every kind big and small
Swimming in schools of hundreds and more
Swans and ducks and goose alike
Shrieking in delight at the sound of trees
As these respond to the gentle push from the winds
The mariners watching in sheer delight
Faces showing they're proud of their town
Their boats moored across the bay
A jetty so small you wonder the need

The market nearby is beginning to thrive
Traders come with all their wares
Music playing from side to side
The quality of which was second to none

We caught their sight as we went along
Some were wondering who the heck we were
Asking questions from all they knew
It seems to me they had a unity of mind
Not unrelated to the peace of the town I think
This big village as old as it is
Is really worth the time we've got

There's that gentle breeze blowing across the field
Schools of pikes scattering in response in the pond
As they gather round to have some prey
It's such a delight to stand aside
As nature plays its tune for us

What about those wooden houses to the right of us
Built of logs that have seen a lot
Their builders seem to have had nature in mind
So it sings the same song as the trees astride

I wish for once the world was like you
Evidence you show that the earth can work
If all abide it shows by the laws of life
Showing respect for things in the world
Reflecting honour for the creations of God

Celle you are great and good it seems
And not because of just your size
But how good are you in truth?
Have you got the boys in hood?
Hidden away in those pretty homes of yours
And the girls that shave their heads like men
Black they wear as if bereaved

They thrive on race and hate of men
Wreaking destruction along their wake

Do these live within your midst?
Tainting the image you created for yourself
Of a land of peace and hope for all
That thrives on good and just and right

Success and perfection is all you want
But still you struggle to shake your past
Of being a land obsessed with hate

I look in you and I saw a man
Terri it was the name of him
He's married to a lady fit and slim
Andy it is I'd call her name
She's slight of nature and never utters a word
But then at home she whacks her man
Screaming at him when none is in sight
Cursing his kit and kin alike
Despite the abuse he wouldn't go away

In orange shirt and jeans
Glasses they both wear in common
But Andy wears hers even at breakfast
There's a sign at the front of the door
The gearbox of a bike in the corner
They do love to bike a lot at speed
Miniature motor bikes in the shelf
Helmets on the rack, sunglasses, gloves and jackets
Same it is with mountain bikes
Expensive ones costing thousands to procure
Scooters parked in their weird garage
They just love the feel of bikes
Every sort of bike is good for them

They also share a love of plants
The love of travel is also shared by both
A map of the world is proof of this
Their favourite topping is the *Nutella* spread

Words of advice they have all the time
Especially on how to deal with the opposite sex
Their relationship with their father in heaven is topmost
Andy is cute, fit and small
Curves at the right places
Terri is tall, big and strong
Masculine in every sense of the word
It seems they have everything in common
Even their love of the outdoors is mutual
Andy has a love of watches
Those cute expensive ones made in Switzerland
Terri loves cute expensive ties
His best passion is for shoes
He's a born leader in body as well as in soul

They've lasted for years
Twenty years in fact they been
So why in the world does happiness escape?
This couple who seem to have everything at their feet
Why does everything never go right for them?
Why do they choose to live as one?
When indeed they are better off apart
Wrinkles of pain lie above their brow
Stretches of agony around their eyes
Because they've chosen against their will

When things go wrong Terri never complains
He'll never cease to try and try
Again and again he'll go in search
Looking round for another style
Unless he resolves the problems at home
Endless they are and never cease
He'll heave and sigh and pant with grief

He talks to strangers upon the street
He chats with the ladies that catch his eye
In search of the friendship he lacks at home
Thinking at least they'll speak to him
The kind of talk he desires from her
His mind wondering what could have been
Had he not entered this bond of endless pain

He imagines sometimes how it could have been
Making love to her the way he really wants
Why I ask has it not worked for them?
Twenty years and still the same
Why on earth do they remain?
When in fact they could have found a way
But the fear of man is very great
That is why they'll remain in pain.

A closer look and I start to smile
Because I behold a couple of a different fate
Kate and Sam I'd call their names
Romeo and Juliet would be put to shame
Seeing the great love between these two
Their life is bliss and happy and secure
They seem to find what most men lack

Kate is round and of no special shape
Even her teeth beggars' belief
Not a piece of them is set
Her hair is short and of brittle kind
Her skin is pale and can never tan
Her waste is round and full of fat
But knowledge she has of how to carry herself
She's got the bounce you have to admit
And her choice of colours is high and great
And then a voice that turns all to gold
She'll never annoy from the sound of her

Sam is different from Terri of course
He's tall and slim and slight by frame
So tall indeed he touches the skies
His charm is zero as indeed his looks
Charisma lacking in every sense
Yet with Kate and suddenly he comes alive
Their bodies flattened together in deep embrace
They have nothing in common at all
Yet respect they have for the other's views

These are the words of Kate to Sam:
'I greet you my great lover and friend
How very kind you have been to me
Through the dark ages you've seen me through
Now indeed I see the light
Now I have my peace of mind
Now I can smile to all again
You've helped me find another me
I had thought for once I'd lost my mind
With you by me my feelings are real
I feel with you I can cope with things
My confidence and hope in life is restored
Because you remained astute right by my side
Through thick and thin you stood so strong
How very kind you have been to me
To me you are worth more than a million stars
May God above bless this awesome love of ours
Blessed be the day that we met for real'

Is this the secret of the success they have
A mutual respect and appreciation of what they've got
How come it works for Kate and Sam?
When it seems to all that shouldn't be the case
Why do Terri and Andy never find their joy?

Only you can tell the answers to these
Being as you are the city of old
Celle you've been there for centuries and more
And recently survived you have of all the blitz.

A pond in Celle, Northern Germany. Look closely and you'll see that there are literally hundreds if not thousands of tiny little green frogs in this pond and they appear to be 'smiling'.

Of Buds and Pests

How could I forget you o great city
How grateful I am to you
I came to you with no escape
That lake of yours called *Balaton*
Tears and pain from a heart that's wrenched
I thought for sure my life was done
That misery and loss would always be my lot
That never again could I force a smile

But then you wouldn't accept my whim
You said to me 'I'll take you in'
With arms of faith you wrapped me in
Across a chest that was broken to bits

I couldn't describe the release I got
The organism of my heart
Loud and forceful then peaceful and calm
Like the quiet you get after a violent storm

It all started when I beheld your borders
From the land of the hills I'd come
A city of ancient operas and theatres
Where recently the sound of music rang out
From where I couldn't find my taste
But the sight of you was just enough
Just what the doctor ordered to ease my pain
At that moment when I needed it the most

A broken heart has walked the entire length of the *Duna*
From *Budafoki* through *Galert* and then *Margit Hid*
Even on that beautiful island tears still flow
Then through the west end to the *Pettofi*
Still the water flowed
The loss of two daughters that are greatly loved

Brought by the appearance of one like the first born
Why is there no one to share my mourn
Why is there no comforter?

Many a time by the riverside
I often wonder about your fate
While I cross the *Poltmalinsky* Bridge
I stop to think where you should be
Where you could be

Many times I wondered aloud
Should I take this life that God gave me?
To jump and plunge upon the rocks beneath

I came to you when I was broken and mashed
You tried your best to sew me up
But then your daughters undid your work
They are the most beautiful of humans
The ones with the most feminine features
But then lack substance enormously
The harshest of all the daughters of men
Hostile to all not their kind
And even those of their kind living without
These visit and then refused to return ever again
These ladies hold the title 'nastiest in all the earth'
Even Nick would be envious of them

They keep putting the visitors off
Often they pour their worst scorn of all
On anyone that catches their fancy
All because they cannot have their way
By the time I left I was more broken than before
Needing again to be stitched together by ones I love

But then where are your men?
Why cannot these just stand up?
Where have they chosen to hide their heads?

There they are between the sheets
Lying within the legs of those beautiful maidens
There in fact they have hidden their brains
No wonder they are so completely dominated
No wonder power deserts them so enormously
Invisible,
Impossible,
Incorrigible
Would they ever wake up?
And for once take up their proper place
A role reserved for men in most nations
Taking their place in the frontline
To lead from the front
To guide a people
Desperate in fact for real leaders

They claim that Prague is beautiful
They should wait until they see Budapest
Flying in bang in the middle of the night
The sight of resplendence becomes your welcome
A view that'll fuel your zest for life
From atop the hills of Liberty

And do come down through the surrounding parks
She's just extraordinarily wonderful
Abundant in bounce and gait
Tasty and elegant
And it's not just the city
Pretty things prancing along busy streets
Street corners that could be much better organised

Especially at summer time
Bottoms gyrating with the wind
Flesh revealed in more ways than one
But then it's also a citadel that's got all things
A centre of learning and culture
Where almost all languages of the world
Learned, mastered and words spoken with ease

A city that's got everything
Without any arrogance at anything
A *varos* that never sleeps
A *fovaros* that is safe to walk
That even night presents no dread
See Budapest and then it is you may die
Much more than the imitation of any other
Not the 'Paris of the East'
But the 'in city' of the world
With no equal at the heart of Europe

Atilla wrote many verses about you
You at one time were the capital of the world
Where the Habsburgs had their feet
Dictating how the world should be run
You even have a tower of your own to match
Although this of yours was not made by man
Neither was it constructed of steel
Not the handwork of a foreign engineer
It's a hill dedicated to the fight for freedom
Overlooking the world from every side
Revealing a city of incontestable beauty

Budapest may not be as green as *Pecs*
May not have the ambience of *Veszprem*
It may not have the homeliness of *Szekes'*
Not the engineering prowess of *Miszkolc*
It may not have the tradition of *Debrecen*
No ancient chapel and round moat of *Jasberenyi*
But this city has a beauty all of its own
With the halo of *Saint Istvan* protecting its lands
It never could and wouldn't be allowed to go wrong

But then I wonder you see
This great city
She has many babies
How could you have a child?
And then throw away its bath water

You deny them the tender care of a mother
They speak the tongue as sweetly as any other
That ethic Hungarian man at *Blaha Lusza ter*
And many more of your children from abroad
From nations that used to be part of you
The greater Hungary that is
They have come from everywhere
You treat then so very cruelly
Even the *Magyar Vizsla kutcsa* is happier
Worse than dogs has been their lot in life
What have they done wrong?
Oh it's because they carry a foreign *ut level*
Slovakia, Transylvania, Serbia and Ukrainia
Why do they all sit around so sad?
With nothing in fact to do
Why are they so miserable?
As despondent as Alonso feels
At Hamilton as he records yet another win
On the formula one circuit

Why have you refused to accept them?
Why do you resist from absorbing them?
Why have you refused to give them jobs?
Then you go around asking for your land back
Asking to have the territories before the Great War
What a joke you post to the world?

You have never spoken with a single voice
Dissention is rampant among your ranks
Is that why it's been so easy to snatch your lands
To have dominion over you
Foreigners raping your girls in frenzy
Over many centuries this has been the case
From Roman times all the way to Soviet days
A history of which you've hidden away
Communist statues rotting away in the shed
Why are you so ashamed of these?

Burying your head and past in the sand
Never willing to confront reality head on
And even now the politicians achieve the same
Exploiting the divisions that seem such a shame

You moan so much about your past
How very hard has been your lot in life
Years of oppression that couldn't be helped
Yet worse treatment you mete out to those
Who come to your shores in search of peace
Especially around *Arpad Hid*
They bring their monies from far and wide
Then you fleece them clean of all their wealth
Stripping them free of all their wares
Then you force them back to where they've come

With plenty they arrive and then empty they return
You promised them loads but then deliver nothing
Hordes of your own kids have even flooded away
To all nations of the world they can be found
What if the nations has been the same to them
Would they have thrived abroad as they've not at home?
Success the kids at home despise and loathe
Black and white could never find a home in you
Because with envy they'll be driven away

Porn has taken a hold of you
Why have you become the headquarters of vice?
Why have you sold your conscience?
Trading your virtue for the sake of pennies
Why do your maidens fleece innocent foreigners?
Selling their precious bodies for a couple of dollars
Why do they deceive with the beauty of their bodies?
Bitching about for a couple of pounds
I hope and pray that this'll change some day
So you can take your place of pride today
Respect for you resounding across the world

The gardens in the forecourt of the Castle in Buda, Budapest, Hungary.

Book III
They Make Life Worth Living

My Teacher, My Father

Let me tell you about my teacher
My teacher is the gentlest, kindest man you will meet
He is soft-spoken with a baritone
His silky velvety voice is a trademark
Even the birds of the skies cannot compete
He is as compassionate as a dotting mother
He is elderly yet so young at heart
Although his hair is all but grey
He is just as fit as a fiddle can be
He touches a thing and it turns to gold
His patience is clear for all to see

He loves to work
He adores his job
He gives his all without restraint
Complete he gives of everything
He delivers without the fear
Of losing all his toiled to have

He is immaculate
He is gorgeous
He is fashionable
He is knowledgeable
He is witty and a lot of fun

Diligence is my teacher's watchword
Humility is his trade mark
People think your greatest love of all is work
But how very wrong indeed they are
Your soul is with your own
Your family is your life
Your heart remains with all of these
Your darling wife from the country of the Danes
Your lovely children of northern descent

Your cute little grand children
How those love the play they have with you
Your beautiful Berliner sister
How much of her you think
And she in turn thinks the world of you

You give at every turn
I never thought the like of you remained
Extinction they thought was the fate of those
Who think and act just like you do
Now I know they're wrong indeed
The truth is that much of your sort abound
A search is done and they are found
Giving the joy that all man craves

My teacher
How very kind you are to me
How very special you've proved to be
You are uniquely designed

I'll tell the world a bit about you
This good man that commands respect
He is self sacrifice itself
His fun is the happiness he gives
Happiness he'll never take from you

How I'll miss you when we leave
How I wish you remain with us
How I wish you never leave
How I crave the permanence of your elegance
But I am keenly aware you have a call
A destiny to which you have set your mind
To protect your own at any cost
Never will you forget your kit
Nor shack your duty by God himself
Your heart is forever with your kin
Exactly where it's supposed to be

You remind me of someone really dear to me
Someone far and far away
In lands where the sun is king
Very similar in kind to you
With skin much darker in fact than you
That one is actually called my dad
You have become a father too
A special role for those who care

I know one day I'll be like you
A clone of you forever more
The heavens know how quick it'll come
How very privileged I then would be
How very nice to wear your shoes
How very happy my life would be
To be called a teacher just like you
A father to all as you have been.

Tower

There is a tower of strength that dwells within
This tower of purpose is here with us
This tower is always there for us
This tower never deserts a friend
This tower will ever make us strong
It is to you I address my talk
How easy it is to talk to you?
How much there is to speak of you

Although you stand so tall
Never afraid of you are we at all
In fact in you we get renewed
Energy and vim at times of great distress
At times of work that never ends
Of stress that never seems to go

It is ever so easy to trust in you
You look so strong and you are that in truth
Solid as a rock not betraying the tenderness within
Powerful enough to resist attack
A shelter at times of need
A cave to hide away from the storm
People run to you and feel really safe
They speak their minds and have no fear
To you the word betrayal simply does not exist

A permanent grin on a face that says
I love only my man and no other one
He's mine and not just a friend
I swore before all men
To be his own for life
And I have his word as well
To be the same to me
To love and own for life

In sickness and in health
Through good and bad times
We follow not the fad
That's common among men today

You love to speak up for yourself
Your mind you bare in full release
To those with whom you feel at ease
To those unkind you'll keep your peace
Speak you wont with those who are uncouth

You blush a lot it seems
Your checks go red when upset
They do the same when embarrassed
All of this is for real
Never to create a spin
To twist the mind around
Deceive you never do

Yes indeed you are shy
But timid never are you
To speak up for your ideas
You speak about your dreams
And none of this is false

A look at you from a distance
And one thinks you frown a lot
But closer to you its clear
That one has been wrong all along
Your face is permanently etched
With a grin that never fades
Your lovely thin little lips
Ever ready to contort into a smile
As shy as you yourself

Walls surround you all about
Some may appear to shine ahead of you
But no regret will you express
Nor allow a grudge to grow
Instead support you still provide
Without a hint of fear or angst
You thread the pathway they have set
With full confidence in them
Cowardice is not your trait
You are bold in everyway

You deserve this lot of yours in life
You've sacrificed so much to be there
Why shouldn't you receive that credit?
Reserved for those who've worked?
Persevered through difficult times

Now at last you've got your wish
To give your life to another being
A little one that grows within
And more of these will come your way
Until you say the word
I've had enough for now

I am sure in months your bike will grow
Like those one sees around in town
With an enclosure attached to its rear
A bambie within its midst
Veiled away from glare
His gleaming wide eyes hidden
With an expression that says I'm proud of mum
Soon you'll have another and another and yet another
Because you deserve the good of life
For all the pains you've had to bear
Over the years as time has gone
What a tower of strength you are?

There's something in you that invites
I'll say this yet again
All men and women to come to you
They come and cut their minds in two
And give to you with certain hope
With them you share their pain and joy
They can't but trust your words
Because sincere you always are
Deceit is the last they'll expect
From a heart that's deep and kind

Your smiles may last but just
A few seconds at a time
But they actually say a lot
They say they are really mean a ton
Its truth that flows from you
You never tell a lie
Or grease the brow of the great
You're not afraid to hurt
As long as you tell the truth

Although you know a lot
You never assume you are right
Your works in years attest to that

Alas you're back again
You part your well shaped mouth
And words of wisdom depart
A deep nice voice that says:
'I'm back and happy to be here
I've missed you all a lot'

Remember that joke a while ago
The one in the midst of the meal
A joke that was not to your taste
You smiled and never said a thing
But the message was clearly received

Never cross my path again
Or I'll crush your toes in two
A giant doesn't have to be brash
But gentle in heart and mind

That is why that one that's yours
Is glowing in sheer delight
He's got a tower in you indeed
A lot that simply is not all men's.

I See You the Way You Are

They all think they know you don't they?
They think you are the hard man of the realm
They think you are without emotion
They think you are without care
They think your heart is dead
They are scared of you

How very wrong they are?
I wish they know you the way I do
The same as those that work with you
You are the most caring of all I've met
You are never scared to admit you are wrong
You are not scared to ask for help
As equal you treat and never ignore
Except some ignorant ones of whom I know

To young and old you have an ear
To pay your dues to all its due
You seek advice from the lowliest of beings
You never do a thing unless it's planned

Although you struggle to speak your mind
Your brain is greater than most of mankind
A genius you are for all to see
The figures you know from back to front
But still consult before you act

You are as clean as crystal
You radiate like diamond
Your tie is always immaculate
On shirts handmade to match your taste
Is this the choice of the judge herself?
Did you ever buy anything yourself?
Or are these the product of the careful search

Of that other half of yours
The feminine one right by your side

They think they know you don't they?
Do they know that you love to laugh?
Do they know that you laugh a lot?
Do they know that you care so much?
Do they know of your love of art?
Do they know of your love of plants?
Do they know that you love the park?

Do they know that you love to live?
Do they know of your love of your own?
Do they know that they command your life?
Do they know that you're not all about work?
Do they know that you love to smile?
At stupid things that make no sense

I know you
You are sensitive
Attractive
A gardener
A perfectionist
You are confident
You are technical
You are sound
You care what others feel
You avoid arguments
You know so much
Yet you love to learn
You love to give
You know your way
You are set in your life
You are a dad
You are a lover

Uppsala! Uppsala! Uppsala! You say
Uppsala! Is never far from your tongue
You say it when you are angry
You repeat it when you make a mistake
You recite it when excited
You chant it when you are happy
Uppsala! You say once again
I'll never know how this is spelt
But my ears have grown so used to it
They'll ever be romanced by the sound they make
Even when we're apart for good

There is more indeed that I see in you
That is why it's true that I love you so.

Northern Star

High above the heavens you stand
Like a firmament in the skies
With envy your mates behold your fame
A great leader knows you well
He said you are constant
And he is right
He said you are of true fixed quality
And yet again he couldn't be more exact
He said there are hardly any like you in the universe
Yet gain one cannot but agree

You are perceived even when you are not seen
You are there even when you have not arrived
Why are you so good northern star?
How could you have come from so far away?
And yet bring so much contentment
How could you have brought so much completeness?

Are you not from the monster?
The hypocrite that is now an empire
The giant that is soon to become history
The worshipper of riches
Who disregards justice and mercy
Disregards humanity
How could such a creature give birth to you?

Alas I say!
You are not an offspring of the beast
You are from the beloved land too small to count
Yet where the beautiful maidens abound
Naïve and fickle in all their ways
The land where the pretty tongue holds sway
The land where the great river flows
Dividing the land in two but one

The land of dreams and great belief
That's where you've really come

Northern star will you be there?
Will joy be yours?
Will peace always own you?
Will peace always descend from you?
Will excitement always flow from you?
Will you be faithful?
Will you be distracted?
Will you speak of your peace as much?
Telling how much of it you care

Will you always be there?
Will you ever go home?
Will you then there remain?

Will you lose your peace?
Will you lose your faith?
Will you lose your hope?
Will you lose your poise?
Will you get sucked in?
Will you become like them?
Will you become jealous?
Will you become envious?

Will you loathe success?
Will you detest achievement?
Will you love mediocrity?
Will you lack excitement?
Will you drive away zeal?

Will you tell your mind?
Without leaving a thing
Will you reveal your pain ?
So you can be helped
Will you start again?

Will you remain in love?
Keeping your word
To live and rest to the limit of your days

A nightingale is what you are
Slim and trim for all to see
Your frame belies the strength within
Stronger than platinum is what you are
Of this a few will ever see

A rock you are and hope you bring
A tower of support to those you love
A helping hand to him that wants
It's such a delight to be your friend

Like a hare in the field you've come to be
You love to ride across the field
Of that bug or more I too I'm caught
We ride in pairs through the countryside
Heaths far away hold no fear for you
No one can hold you when you're resolved
They can't but follow the lead you laid

Respect you will get wherever you go
Because deserved you are of things that are good
You are great indeed you star from the north

Here Lies the Lady

This lady I want to talk about
This lady is very special indeed
Not at all by the world's standards
She didn't have lots of money
She probably didn't have lots of jewellery
Neither did she have a big house
Nor myriads of friends

All she had was a big heart
All she had was a big smile
All she had was a big voice
All she had were a few packs
Packs of cigarette dangling from her right hand
All she had was her wine glass

The unwary will only remember you
But the discreet will realize too quickly
That you are much more than these
A woman of substance like any one else
A mother of two who's proud of hers
Even these have one or two of there's
Did anyone really care about you?
At that hour when you could be saved
What a shameful world we've come to have?
Where one lives and dies as no one cares

How could such a kind lady as you fall?
Fall asleep in silence without a word
How couldn't the world have heard you scream?
A shout for help from a heart that's sick
A heart that hurts and aches like mad
Could this be the pain that took your voice?

How could somebody as kind as you
Die the death so quiet and unannounced
Not for you, you were too kind
To lie helpless in that great heat
Without a care and a help at all
Three days indeed you there laid still
Until one who cared so much was there to help
A very special friend he's been to you
But even he by then was late

To many of us you were a mum
An aunt that hugs us without restraint
Who says hello with a deep strong voice
Who loves to play with one and all
That is why we will never stop to say our words
You are a special lady to us for hey
And that you'll remain forever more.

Tribute

Dear Aunty,

You didn't know us and yet you showed so much kindness. You were genuinely interested in all of us. You took us like your sons and daughters and we began to look upon you as our mum.

I in particular am filled with sorrow when I remember you.

I remember you hugging me so many times with your lovely cigarette stick hanging from your right hand. You are so much fun.

A few days before you passed away, you invited me into your flat. You insisted I must come in. Then you showed me all your family portraits, you told me the story of your life and gave me a few shots of *palinka* (Hungarian name for gin) to wash it all down.

I never realized that you were actually saying goodbye. I cry everyday because I wonder if you could have been saved had anyone noticed that moment when you fell ill. I ask myself did I do everything I could? Could I have saved you? I know now that there is virtually nothing anyone could do. There probably was not much pain because you died within seconds. Thank goodness for that.

You are the second of mine that this disease has killed. The first was my biological mother; she was only 38 years old.

I thank God for your life.

I am sad at your sudden death Aunty especially because your body lay in that room for 3 days until our beloved friend Balazs discovered you. It is not befitting for someone as kind as you. You were just too nice for that. I however take consolation in the fact that you brought joy to me and many others.

God bless you Aunty and may you live forever in his kind memory. May the light of the memory of you never quench.

Lots of love from me,

Tony, Tony.

The Rock of Jenningham

In a land very far away
Many years ago

There was born a ruddy rock amidst the sea
Comely in fact of appearance
Of soft surface, the feminine type
Fresh and cuddly and beautiful
These were days as many as the lifespan of a man
The seas were warm gentle and beautiful
Blue, calm and bright and cloudless skies
This was a day of celebration and excitement
Laughter and joy from all around
In a land where music still survives
Colonies Jamming with the reggae beat
Played with the fumes of burning weed
The king of the bush carnal in its bliss
Hips gyrating to a regal beat
Legs hopping up and down as if possessed
Smoke drifting from the noses of the masters
Eyes glazed and red like fresh blood

Not very long after this birth
The rock was moved to another place
By share force of nature
A fight for succession
And the opportunity came for a new lord
The Angles came and have made it their own
Thrived they have in bounds upon this grove
Where they manage to leap but without a smile
There the rock now has the care
Of children she never bore
For people she doesn't know
But daunted not she took to her role
And made this foreign clime a lovely home

72

Why is the world contending over you?
Nations battling to be your sovereign
Kev of the inns being the governor general
Don't they all realise that to him you belong?
And would always be whatever the odds
He may not be the tallest of rocks
Never claiming to be the strongest of all
But sworn you have and so shall be
To be his own and so for life
All because of your love for the Divine
A dedication of your heart and adoration
And astute you are of that solemn oath

Why do you insist on compliance?
With a regulation that denies the right to joy
Which restrains the right to begin again?
An entitlement to peace of mind
That every kind of man should have
To fall and fail then stand and start afresh
Rebuilding a life that's lost then found anew
Under a roof that is free from strife
Like spring heralds the dawn of life
As lilies bloom at the sight of the rain

Carnations flourish atop of you
Your branches are spread as high as the skies
Like the ancient pine trees of Rome
That witnessed the massacre of the saints
They are still alive to tell the tale
These trees are free for all to roost
The chicks of the world can come to lie
On the single condition they are true and plain
Because if not they'll be sent on their way
Not in the nicest of ways
Never to receive the chance again

You walk and talk like a Caribbean queen
Levitating in the air like the Pope in Rome
Or more I'll say like brother Majella
Not for pride but only in faith
Humble you are but not a fool

Sometimes you feel not like a rock
More like the jelly of the stock
But your strength is strong and lies within
You remain as hard as Italian bread
Let them try you and soon they'll see
The power will come from up above

Now that Don the great is gone
God bless him and all his own
Seems the traitor is now the one
That fellow with the thick moustache
His head shinning like the cathode tube
To read the Psalms on the day of your bed
I hope and pray by God above
That he lives not to see the day
Because no back-stabber should have your glory
Your thunder belongs to you and you alone

I wonder very often
How could you have survived?
How you managed to fly so high above the clouds
Well away from the opposing crowd

When your caravan passes they start to ache
You drive along and their depression starts
You pray in white and their sky is grey
When all and sundry want to use your head
To drink their wine in the middle of the night
How could you have thrived so well?
Complete with your flora and fauna too
Even with your silvery horse in tow

Surrounded as you are on every side
By sharks, piranhas and shoals of dangerous fish
Snipers and devourers and destroyers
They've laid a siege everywhere
They wish everyday to see your doom
Cursing and wishing for bad to no avail
To have your bones crushed between their teeth
Gnarling aloud to no end

They sit around there looking so sad
As despondent as Alonso feels
At yet another of those Hamilton wins
On the famous formula one circuit

Yet their failure is evident for all to see
They'll never have your flesh for dinner
Because you have the perfect watchman
Your creator has chosen to guide your path
Special is the way he feels for you

Believe it a not
Even the gentlest of giants can be roused
And would slap you down when provoked
Without regard to what could be wrecked
Threatening to consume all in its wake
The most precious of all relationships
Freedom not compromised for anything
Absolutely true it is of this rock of old
Maybe this was what scared the little girl
The little cute thing with saucer eyes
Her dark brown skin gleaming with innocence
You called her and she wouldn't respond
Blatantly refusing to be cuddled by you
And when prompted for her reason
With a little cute voice she replied:
"Because I am scared"
Her frightful eyes and her shivering body

Speaking much louder than her voice could
But should she really be in fear of you?
How very wrong she was of course?
Because this rock of mine never hurts anyone
Nor anything not even a common fly

Rocks abound in the open sea
But you stand tall above the rest
Swimming around you are dolphins of every kind
Laughing and joking as they thrive in your shallows
Because you are ever ready to protect your own
Ever ready for the course you chose

You do have doubts about your faith
Not uncommon to all mortal men
But misgivings are locked away within your heart
More than the clock for accuracy you are
Sitting in that favourite chair come rain come shine
In your assigned place of steady service

You know the writings back to front
And yet remain silent in a congregation of parrots
Letting good deeds do all the talking
Faith held strong and unwavering
Despite years of isolation
Several decades of humiliation
You retain the peace that only comes from God

In Africa your foundations were laid
In the Caribbean you were conceived
But now in Europe you've come to live
And there it is you've made you home

For years you were trained to care
For decades you cared for all
Now rest you have from all your works
Now for others to care for you
Just as much as you have done

Others may play the ding dong game
But firm indeed you stood your ground
Steady and still compared to diamond
Steadfast for sure as the rock you are

The Barbary monkeys have made a home in you
One of them is Mark of the horses
The other is Nad of the deans
She has brought a mate of another species
Another not borne has made you his
He is well toned and walks to bliss
God has his own unique ways doesn't he?
How he does things that man cannot fathom
He even provides a mum for the motherless

One contacts you and progress hits them
To you regression never fits
Yet concession you make as deemed fit
Only to those deserving of trust

Your accolades are proclaimed in the skies
A beacon you've become for all to see
Acclaim given well above the 'levante' clouds
You may be old but youth is still in your mind
A lion heart that never shakes
Plastic knees nonetheless
Your focus is always on what's ahead
Never for once dwelling on the past
And that is why I see the mass of men
Courting you like nobles do with charm
All because of the honesty and truth in you

Two thousand pounds is big to them
But to you it's but a few humble coins
You may be a pensioner
In poverty you'll never live

At day you glow like the sun
And at night your reflection is just as the moon
Although you are a rock
Never will you go amuck
Your bag is full held aloft with peace
Controlled you are in every place
Never for once to bring a strain
Never here to cause one pain
Forever more will this be the case

O how much your eyes have seen o rock
And look how well of all you've thrived

Epilogue

It took a while to write my lines
But here I am and here to stay
Within you heart I've found a place
And a love of you resides in me
Our paths have crossed
Uncrossed they won't

Only one single vow I ask from you
One single request I'll make of you
That as God lives you will be there
That you won't submerge back into the sea
To the deep from which you sprang
Until the third daughter is released to us
Then at last we have not one but two Winnies
A second rock that ever wins.

Book IV
These Ones You'd
Rather Forget

Silvery Eyes (Crystal)

I keep beholding you all the time
What really indeed are you?
Are you a great friend or a formidable foe?
A competitor or co-operator
Do you like or do you dislike?
Do you love or do you despise?
Do you admire or do you loathe?
Are you loose or are you tight?
Are you cold or are you hot?
Where really do you stand?

You claim to love nothing at all
That work means nothing to you
But is this really the way you feel
Or are you telling these to grease our brows
Is it true that work really means your life?
That your ambition burns like fire
A mad inferno that could never be quenched
That you'll trample on any that blocks your way
That you love to hate at every turn
That you do distrust all that come your way
Not even your friends in fact escape

No one can know what to say to you
Is jealousy that deep within your veins?
Do you despise just because you cannot compete?
Do you dislike for sheer delight?
Complain you make of everything
Not even to yourself are you ever kind
You'll never reveal what's deep inside
That heart of yours that's closed to all
Will you for once reveal your thoughts?
That sanguine poise that means to kill

Who in fact do you admire?
Do you really love as you claim to do?
Why on earth do you pretend?
To be close to those that are close to you
Your closest friends are fast and stylish
They attire themselves as models do
Bouncing about like antelopes in the Masai Mara

Like a snake so green you hide yourself
Among the blades you've made your home
To sting and hurt at anytime you choose
You have the skin that men die for
Yet its you alone that doesn't take a note

To you one cannot tell
All we see are your blue piercing eyes
Questions they ask but answers they'll never give
The beauty of them no one can doubt

You have the waist that most admire
Yet you won't but kick against the thing
Your gait is fast yet your style is unknown
Your choice of colours is sheer delight
Your skill is clear no doubt exists
Talent immense without a dissent
Yet you'll never admit to what you can do
Never sharing the knowledge you possess

Is there a chameleon among the leaves?
Hiding itself from all of us
Where indeed do you belong?
Are you a star or just a shadow?
A comet or just a meteor
Are you a camel or a horse?
It's up to you to decide your lot
Have you been hurt or it's just your dream?
Will you be kind to all one day?

To open your heart for all to see
And then at last your beauty behold.

Those silvery blue eyes of yours
How very delightful a sight they make
Hidden they are by a frown all day
The brows that squeeze in sheer distress
Hiding a shadow of confusion from deep within

Your voice,
Angelic they are in their sound and pitch
Like the choir above they sound to the ears
There's no tongue that could hide your tone
All will know of your central roots
I just hope that sometimes you can mean your smile

Your heart resides with one at home
That grand old one that loves you so
With eyes as blue and bright as yours
As cute as you but joy reflects

Your teeth is clean every time of the day
A result of the constant care and attention you give
Even then you still have a wish
You'll never rest until just as white
As enamel itself you want them so
Always reaching for perfection you do
In the most unimportant of issues to man

Who really are you I ask again?
Time will tell the answer to that

Everything you see is bad
Everyone you meet is wrong
You have a word of scorn
As soon as you open your mouth
Except for the men that dress in blue

The land that flirts with the deep blue sea
Their curls brown as their eyes are too
To them your cravings will always lie

You treat others as bad as you treat yourself
There is such a sting within your voice
You jump on those that are not your tribe
All their speech is watched by you
To trip them up as you desire
Or to speak against them at every turn
Even though they've come from far away
To make a home of this fair land
But those of your tribe can never be wrong
Even vagrants of those are saints to you

Tears are not very far away from your eyes
They give a feeling you do really care
Where are these emotions of yours from?
Especially from you of all mankind
One that holds a grudge with everyone
Most of which is without a cause

Your skin glows and gleams in the sun
Tan as bronze polished with oil
Just as the trees gleam in response to day break
Providing perfect foreground for the horizon
Especially at mid summer
But you, only you will be last to behold

Your jaws are admirable in size and setting
Immaculate in every way
Yet to you they need some job
'They are not attractive enough' you say to all.

You are a prototype of your kind at home
Beauty they have extensively
Guts they lack enormously

Confident they look in everyway
But none indeed of it possess
Envious they feel for all that's good
Jealous they are of everyone
Of anyone that does the right.

With bitterness and hate you live your days
How on earth would they be long?

Your sting is worse than a scorpion's
Your mouth is sharp like a double-edged sword
Mostly when it wants to criticise
Never in life does it commend
Never does it give
Nothing positive will come from you

You are in fact a sniper
With guns ablaze to shoot at will
The unbeguiled that lose their guards
With sheer delight you respond to this
It's the only source of confidence you have
This killing at will of those ill and weak

Epilogue

In hope.

Suddenly it dawned on me
How quickly the scales fell away
Removed I did the screen
And I could see beyond the clouds

I thought I knew you well
Little indeed I did behold
All I saw was just a façade
Now I can see your beauty and poise
The perfect skin that glows in the sun
The smile that comes but just a few
How very small of the battles behind I saw
How hard it is to be yourself
How tough to deal with what you are

You have a fear that sits within
A panic deep inside the bones
A pain from the past that never heals
The loss of one that means so much
One whose place can never be filled
One whose love none can replace

How very hard life can be
When everyone seems to be a star
But the real star remains ignored
In the shadow dark and lonely
So much noise about
And yet so much quiet deep inside
How hard in truth you tried.

The wind comes and blows away your sail
Never letting show the sailing skills
But strong you must remain to stay afloat
You'll never sink with all your work
Unless of course it is indeed your wish
I hope and pray it's not the way for you
This silent star that stays ignored.

How Can I Be Your Friend

How can I be friends with you?
When you want to gun me down
When all you feel for me is hate
When your mind to me is dark
When you want to take my lot
When you speak so bad about me so
When I look at you and see dislike
When you talk behind my back
When all you see in me is faults

How can I be friends with you?
When I gave you all that I've got
When I stood by you through thick and thin
All the time that no one dared
When I cared for you
Even when I was so tired
When I left my bed to be with you
When I showed concern above all else
When I followed you everywhere

How the heck could I ever be your friend?
When you told the world all that we shared
Opening to all our confidential talk
Here I am keeping my peace
All your secrets one and all
Carrying them deep inside my soul
Never revealed to the day I die

How do you think I'll be your friend?
When your every wish for me is bad
Hoping soon I'll be destroyed
Despite the truth I held you close
Cradling your face gently in my arms
Wiping away the sorrow of your heart
Spat at by others you called your own

Never chance to risk again
Being close to you alone
Nor dare to speak my heart again
With friends like you there's none a friend

Why Shouldn't I Love Her So?

I find myself asking this question
In recent days this question has romanced my mind
Could I ever have an answer to this obvious question?
Especially as you've taken so much away from me

You were given the regard and respect befitting a queen
Yet you responded in the manner of a tramp
You have ignored courtesy and love and respect
You have insisted on having it all your way
You wouldn't even give out of what was got
Why should anyone want to be with you?

I think I have an answer to this
I like you so much from deep within
Because your beauty surpasses all being
Also because of your gentle calm disposition
I like you because of your apparent kind heart
I like you because of your bright green eyes
I like you because of the sunshine you bring
I like you because of your willingness to listen
I like you because you love to learn

I like you because you never raise your voice
I like you because of the peace that surrounds you
I like you because of your disarming smile
I like you because you exhume trust
I like you because you promise so much

I like you because of your succulent luscious body
I like you because of your supple breasts
I like you because of your set white teeth
I like you because of your deep brown hair
Long they are as all through your spine
Reaching all the way down to your butt

Oh your bottom, what beauty the sight of them!
They are cute, curvy, shapely and elegant
And by heaven don't you know how to move them?
One wonders why your pelvis is so unique
And your front how so delightful
Well trimmed you are always hoozing a delightful smell
They sit on legs that are as lovely as they are shapely
These move so regally as if you have no bones in them

But should I really love you so?
When just a few days after our most intimate times
It's your habit to go into bed with another one
Who bounces you about like a rubber ball.

How did I meet you?
How did I come to invite pleasure into my life?
Followed almost immediately with unhappiness and misery
Who will save one from this canker that you have become?
That has eaten deep inside my bones?
Now let me tell you this my tale

We met together that October day
On the mechanical snake that travels under the ground
One that carries humans from place to place
Blue it was as the deep blue sea
You were sitting adjacent in black
Big these were so I couldn't see you as much
One couldn't notice your hair as well
Because they were tied back high above your neck
All I could see was just your face
It was warm, inviting, friendly and nice
Hosting greyish green eyes that looked a little concerned
I shouldn't have looked too much should I?
I should have let it go straight away
But I didn't give up looking at you,
I was already smitten right from the start

We got off at that same place
I needed direction and asked if you could speak the tongue
And you very kindly replied 'yes of course I will try'
It was the gentlest kindliest reply I've ever heard
And true to it you showed me the way
How thoroughly deceived I was
What a chameleon you are indeed
How so very deceptive you showed yourself
Like that green snake that lies unseen
But whose very venom is worse than a viper sting

Had I known I should have walked away
But the foolish one in me had taken over my brain
Quickly it asked if you had a man
You said yes and that it only just begun
You told me about your family
You told me what you did for a living
I asked if you would love to meet
Just as a friend I said 'no sex' I emphasised
'Yes of course' you said in that soft gentle lovely tone
This time around the time was fixed
The place was determined to meet with you

I shouldn't have been there that day should I?
Had I known the disaster that will follow from it
The misery that will befall me through your hands
Had I known you will provoke him to return?
That evil one that lives in me

Had I known you were so deadly
I should have walked away for hey
If I had known what deadly poison you were

Why should I like you?
Why should I not hate you?
I thought you were so human
I should have known you were hard

Unfeeling indeed like a stone
I should have known you were a heartless destroyer
Had I known you were so unstable
Had I known you will always come and go?
Had I known you will always sleep around
Had I known you will break my heart
Over and over as it pleases you
I should have stayed well clear of you
What an incurable cancer you are

Do all your boyfriends hate you so?
Do all your lovers despise you much?
Do they loathe you for your eccentric behaviour?
Is that why you are so concerned?
Is that why you sulk so much?
Is that why you crave acceptance?
Is that why you are so scared?
I should have stayed well clear of you
What a destroying disease you've proved to be?

Now back to that second meeting
I wonder what was going through your mind
What it was you were thinking about
'Did you think this one is cute?
This dark one could speak the tongue
This new one could be of use
To speak the tongue that I long to speak
This traveller could help me and my love
To travel the world as we would have liked
Maybe this fellow will be good in bed
Better than the one I had before
I don't have to do anything with him
I'll just keep him at bay from me
I'll just be careful and not get close
I never once will commit my heart'

As for me my thoughts were great
Suddenly I recognised the truth about you
You were the girl I saw in my dreams
The previous week before the last
The one girl I told my friends about
With long hair that reached the waste
Very tall with grey green eyes
Could it be that dream was from up above?
Could this be from the Holy One himself?
Dismissed I did of these strange thoughts
No good girls exists at home
Frivolous they are and reliable they are not
One and all they come and go
Like the rain that falls on the Isle of Mann
That you couldn't be different from these your peers

How very wrong indeed I was
We met for tea and then were stuck
Like twins co-joined from above the chest
Our fates were linked of this I knew
Our happiness dependent upon the other's

It was early evening the following week
Just a week after the first time we met
You had a light beige pull over
It hid your beautiful olive green shirt
On jeans trousers bleached almost white
You smiled at me from the escalator
That golden smile that has become your mark
I couldn't miss them for all the world

I kissed you on both your cheeks and hugged you close
Asked of you how you have been
In response you smiled some more
It was the sweetest gentlest of the best kind
That's how deceptively convincing you are

We walked down that street that leads to home
Eventually getting to near my flat
We got straight into the room
You sat on the bed and folded your legs
Hugging the pillows as if they are kids
You said you'll leave at the stroke of seven
Eventually you didn't leave until well beyond
It was an evening of delightful conversation
We talked about everything
While looking deeply in each other's eyes
Then as you got up to go
I brought your present from the land of the queen
It was the first of many that came to you
An emerald green necklace on silver chains
You wouldn't accept it for all its worth
It was the first of many refusals
Then persuaded you put it around your neck
Pulling away your long hair to give them place
You went to see yourself in the mirror
And remarked how beautiful you thought they were
You kept it on your neck the rest of the night
That was the very last time I'll see these pearls
Then you left the room
Then I saw you off to the station
Kissed you goodnight with a promise to be back
And you kept this promise of yours
As it turned out you rarely ever break any promises
Unless that mad streak of yours
That shows up from time to time

After you left I thought how very pretty you were
How very well behaved you've proved to be
I began to see you as very special
How wrong I was?
I should have walked away that instant
But my stupid half was beginning to hold sway
It was beginning to like you
It was getting to entrap itself

Now how about that third meeting
It was one of many
It was the beginning of the madness that came from you
Before going into the detail of this meeting
Let me tell of an uncanny coincidence
This was how you managed to churn up my brain

On the day I met you I was looking for a job
On the day of your first visit I got that job
My stupid brain immediately took this as an omen
It assumed that all you will bring is good
How very wrong it was for sure

This coincidence was just that
All you will bring is destruction
All you will bring is devastation
All you will bring is desolation
All you will bring is decapitation
What a shame it took so long to realise

Back to that third meeting again
As usual we met at our favourite stop
At that appointed time of five o clock
This time around I couldn't remember what you wore
But I know must have been smart as you always are
We flirted like mad as we head for home
A meal of pasta was made as well
You ate the meal and had some wine
Then merry you became like never before

Then it was we started to play
I said to you I like you a lot
To which you replied you felt the same
I started to stroke your beautiful long hair
Taking the strands around my hands
Then I started to play with your breast
All the while with music in the background

Soft cool songs that relax the mind
At one point I remember you saying there was blood
That if I didn't mind that you don't object
I was too carried away to stop myself
We got the rubber out and began the show
All your clothes you pulled yourself
Yet another trend that will continue with us
I couldn't stroke you crotch because of the blood
But I remember sucking on your breast very hard
Eventually we consummated the love we felt
Penetrating into you in a sweet nice way
We made the most gentle beautiful sex as indeed there were
Softer and softer at first to the beat of the song
Never tiring of ourselves in bed
Climax upon climax we experienced together
Until it was time for you to go
This was yet another trend with the two of us

After this you put on your clothes
Elegantly and organised this action of yours
Went straight back to the bathroom to clean yourself
Sometimes I wonder what it is you do
Because immediately you returned smelling fresh
As if perfumed from head to toe
As if reborn from what we did
Like a new born baby in the maternity ward

Only by now your attitude had changed
The feeling of tenderness is all but gone
You no longer want to be touched nor kissed
This was another trend that continued with us

This meeting took place two weeks after we met
You looked happy and then you were sad
Betrayed you have of the boy you loved
You didn't want anymore of this 'our thing'
No matter how sweet it must have been

You didn't want anymore you said again
That we must never go this way again
To this I agreed and gave my word
But told you that I really liked you
Will not want to lose you at all
It seems my body certainly likes your body
You agreed that you'll visit another time
By now it was clear I was going to travel away for months
I wanted to spend a lot of time with you
I wasn't sure you weren't sleeping around
I was soon to find you out

Your visits were now becoming very frequent
Twice a week mostly
We were due out to see the town
You came as arranged in the morning at ten
As soon as you arrived you sat on the bed
It was obvious you didn't want to go out at all
Not with me for day or night
Instead on this we made love all day
I couldn't count how many sessions we had
All I remember was the music playing between
By the time we finished we were aching all around
We promised again to meet in days
You arrived later than arranged
You didn't call to say you'll be late
Your eyes wide open as they were stern
With deep real frowns in the fore of your head
You wouldn't smile as was usual with you
You said you wouldn't be staying at all
You left immediately as soon as you arrived
No goodbyes, no smiles and certainly no explanation
That was the last I saw of you that weekend
This was the devastating trend that was to continue
I should have been warned
Was I sleeping with a crazy woman?

I know another reason why I liked you so much
It was the result of another sheer coincidence
Before I met you I had lost faith in men
I had learned never to trust friends
I had abandoned my spirituality
I had decided never to profess faith
Never to be part of any religion
But my unquenchable love for God remained
Stronger now that it's ever been
My relationship with the Almighty become close
Closer than I've ever felt before

When you came into my life that October day
And remained in my life
A new calmness came over me
Your vulnerable and calm countenance made me aware
It made me aware again of my spiritual side
I began to have a craving for fellowship
I began to trust in men again
My trust started to grow on you
And before I knew it I was back in church
How yet again I was wrong
Thoroughly misled one more time
I thought you brought God back in my life
All you will bring is misery, deception and decay
What a fraud you prove to be

Now let me talk about that fateful day
The day our delightful friends came calling
The day we had a sudden visit to our room
While we were in the throng of passion

You came early that day
Sat down as you do across the bed
Legs crossed and folded below your waist
And it wasn't long that our bodies began to react
We kissed a little

I love to kiss but sometimes you don't
This all depends upon you mood
I would never understand why your kiss disappears
It evaporates as quickly as you do
I guess nothing about you is really certain
That day we've had a couple of sessions
It was all going so sweet
Then the doorbell rang
It was in the middle of the day
Our friends have arrived as they have planned
We paid no attention the two of us
But the friend at home opened to them
Our friend wasn't told we were in the room
He badgered straight ahead into the room
Saw us two in a beautiful state
He shuddered and fretted at the sight of us
Feigning shock while begging to leave
We'll never know what happened to him
Was it curiosity that got the better of him?
We still continued to make our love
When we're done we slipped into our clothes
Welcomed our friends and the party began

You were so uneasy, tense and nervous that day
But a few beers down and your nervousness was gone
You began to smile and spoke your mother tongue
With our female friend an alliance you formed
For once she thought how genuine indeed you are
But you know for sure it was just another lie

We drank and danced
Then we laughed and started to play fight
As twilight approached we set about town
We needed to crown the evening with a delightful meal
To the French quarter of town we went
All four of us
We wanted a Mediterranean meal

To spice up our evening
But all the tables were taken
We couldn't have the crowning glory we wanted
It had to be put off for the next day
We re-arranged to meet the following day
You were to come to the flat
The next day came and you couldn't be found
We waited by the phone but you didn't call
We tried to call you but you couldn't be reached
We soon realised you were back again
Your insanity had now prevailed
Your heart had turned to stone again
You have brought pain to your friends again

I remember you saying you shouldn't be loved
You don't deserve any kind words you say
You always bring pain to the ones who loved you
Isn't that why they hate you so?
That same destruction has been my lot
How very nice that I couldn't learn
I was so deaf to take a note
Too blind to see the sign
Too dumb to perceive the warning
It's such a shame it happened to me

Why should I not be in love with you?
Why should anyone not be crazy about you?
When your repertoire is full of tricks
Even your dad is fooled by you
A virgin untouched he thinks you are
Although of this I have my doubts
So many lies like this you've told
It could jolly well be one of your tricks
A common lie you tell to all
To all who care to give their ears

I'll tell another occasion you used your tricks
Three or four times of this I do recall
You had once again mysteriously sensed my need
You had known I needed a friend
You had known I hated to be alone
And so a plan you hatched so smooth
A scheme that seemed to work so well
A path straight to the heart of the innocent

I suggested we met up once
You had sensed how important it was to me
You met me at the port for machines that fly
The first time you met me I was so impressed
I was coming home from the motherland
The land of the queen that smiles so thin
A smile of which she never means
Then it was you waited again
Patiently waiting for hours on end
How I was full of praise for you indeed
The third time you pulled a trick or two
You had observed my love for pillows
You had guessed I love them in all shapes
When you met me this third time
You had this cute copper coloured pillow in your bag
It had the sign that clearly says 'friends forever' we shall remain
Was it yet another lie or just a trick
That led you straight inside my heart
A place you stayed until I found you out
I found out you were just a slot
You'd used your tricks many times before
And since it's so successful you wouldn't stop
Never to halt until you're done
Done by a love that hates you much
Hates you so for all you've done
The wicked ways that have become
I'll tell again of yet another trick

In a while I will commence
I've told already your trick with books
Why you chose to do them so
You're quite aware of my love of books
Books were my way of life
You knew also about the love of the new land
You knew how I wanted to speak
The native tongue that tickles the ears
Only spoken by the beautiful maidens
And so again your tricks were at work
You bought a book of tongues for me
It was just a loan you said at first
You never received the money that was due
Was it just another trick?
To make me think you were so kind
When in fact you were a wrecker
When in fact you were a witch
A witch that destroys the peace
A witch that hates to hear of God
A witch that hates whatever is good

How very ashamed I am of me
That I got involved with you at all
That I allowed you to trick me so
All the while thinking you were true to me
You had friends without a name
You had sex at your own free will
Without care to who you hurt
Without concern for what it does
Without a care of the destruction it'll wrought
As long as it gets you the high you crave
That release that you seek always
The grass is always green on the other side
In every plot that's not your own

You hop yourself from bed to bed
Even frogs are left behind in your wake
Neither are locusts fast enough as you
You will use at your free will
You will depart the scene as soon as you come
Leaving destruction and misery in your wake
Misery to those you chance to meet

Why on earth should I love you?
When the demon in me hates you
He's the one that gets at you
The very one possessing the sting
That very one that makes you cry
The only one that can break your heart

Now I'll tell you about this demon
He the very one who is the opposite of me
He started out as my means of escape
Today he is my avenger of wrong
He dares to say the words I can't

The demon started out as a child
He was a little girl at first
He was in fact a creation of mine
A devise to deal with stress
When I was young I never cried
Never cried because I needn't do
My father never cried as long as I know
And only once did I see my mother cry
All my kin were a happy bunch
Although we had our times of need
We faced them all with guts and glee

But when I met the wicked one
A bully like who you'll never be
A copy of who you'll never become
Although just as deadly as you've proved to be

Death dealing and stinging as you've turned to be
Selfish and mean as no one can
She never learnt to give at all
She only gave abuse and curse

I couldn't escape her abuse and scorn
And as I never learnt to cry at all
So I never did relieve my stress
This little girl came and rescued me
At first she cried in secret alone
Then she learnt to cry for me
She would appear in response to abuse
And would help relieve my pain

She would cry at every turn
She didn't mind where on earth indeed she did
Even then the abuse persists
Then it was the girl began to grow
She changed a lot as time went on
Metamorphosed she did into a deadly one
A demon mean and mad as she never was
One who knew how naïve I'd been
He knew how stupid his creator had been
So the opposite of him he changed himself
A loud demon with the sting of a viper
With red hot anger flowing through his veins
One who can give as much as he takes
He's not afraid of abuse at all

Although he's rude and crude indeed
He knows you much more than I could do
He is keenly aware of the deceit in you
He can see through your rocky heart
He can penetrate your fake innocence
That is why he treats you so
Like the tramp he's convinced you are
I will never speak the way he does

But grateful I am that he's there for me
Happy that he's come to reveal your being
Grateful he's shown you up the way you are
Projecting your image as it truly was
Singling you out for his anger and vex
Because he realises you're just a fake
That no matter how many promises indeed you make
You'll never keep a word of yours
You'll never desist from telling a lie
He knows what you are all about
That your existence is to take and take
Taking the treasures that the world could provide
From everyone that you stumble to meet
Everything that you chance upon
To give misery in return for good
Bringing devastation at all your path
To deprive peace at times of need
At every turn you'll not relive

What a shame you've come to be
How very glad I feel again
To be finally rid of the disease that's you
How very grateful to him I am
That he made me realise you shouldn't be loved
For exposing you as the fraud you are
The craziness that lives within your brain
The madness you display all of the way
The lie you tell always
How very grateful I am to him

I continue my tale from where I stopped
I sit by a lake that was dug by man
By a man that was truly great in every way
Who led a nation that was grand and in need
Instead he turned then into a giant in rage
His mind was evil from top to down
As evil as now most of all mankind

Let me tell of another deceit by you
That turned my mind like a little child
I should have been warned but took no heed
You pretended as if you didn't know me
Never for once did you draw near
Instead you chose to skate alone
For a time you chose to skate with a friend
He got to talk to you a lot
He spoke to you to draw you out
You said to him you weren't in love
That never forever will you be in love
That all you were was using me
That I was indeed not of your type
All of this and more you said to him
So why did you accept to spend the evening with us
What baffles one is what you did
Not quite long from these you said
How shameless indeed you are

Friends remarked your heart is closed
How very right they were indeed
Because in truth your heart is stone

You would have become my own
You would have been my girl indeed
You would have become my woman for life
But that in fact was another lie

I gave up on you at last
So I decided to go my way
This time around to be on my own
To find the peace that all people yearn
The peace that stays for all the time
And yet again I found my peace
The strength that dwells within the being
I had once again learned to live and love
To live and love the life I had

I started to cruise in words and deed
Even the birds of heaven soon found me out
They came to perch on my lovely fence
I thought for once I'm free of you
How very wrong indeed I was
I never will let you back in my heart
I'll never show you the way to me
But you had my heart and I cannot leave
What a fool I'd been again
You'll soon destroy this peace I found
Your selfish ways were back again

It didn't take long before you came
By magic you've sensed this peace in me
You had missed the things you got from me
Those expensive presents that make you smile
You had learned from friends I have a home
And yet again your greed is back

You were back on the phone to me again
Asking for me to be your friend
This 'thing of ours' you said to me
Will it forever and ever remain?
I said to you I'd found my peace
And couldn't find a reply to that
Then you plotted a wicked ploy
Why you did it I couldn't tell
Was it because you found I could live again?
Without you and with no regrets
Was it the fact of my brand new home?

Your ploy was to send your mum to me
Be laden with presents for you through me
To me also she brought some gifts
To me she said the kindest words
And words of thanks she never spared

I got the gift that's meant for you
To you I phoned to take your gifts
You won't agree to meet on the street
Instead you begged to meet with me
To spend the weekend with my kit and kin
I never knew you were up to your ways
As soon as you came your smile was back
This time as cool and calm as these can be
My bottom was a rest for your crafty palm
As tender you were as never before
With promises of change you made to me
You'll never return to the way you were
That you'll never break my heart again
That this time you're here to stay
To stay and live forever more
How very sad you are indeed
To fool around the way you do
To trick a man that cares for you
What a shame you are indeed

That is how you came to be
To sleep in the bed you shouldn't have slept
To spend the weekend where you didn't belong
To show love as if you're real
To meet those you shouldn't have met
To meet with hearts that were yet to mend
You went indeed to the sea with them
The beach was yours for another day
Seeing yet again those beautiful sights
In the most lovely of southern shores
Eating meals that were made of dreams
The kind you never have had before
There was one who saw you through
That complex you appeared to her
That trust for you should come with time
Maybe that's the reason you couldn't call
To say thank you was not to be

That is how you repay kindness
What an ingrate you are indeed
That same treatment will come my way

You hadn't quit your wicked ways
Despite all the promises you gave again
You managed this time to trick and deceive
With words I now know were never meant
I love you was all you said
Despite the fact you had your boys
The H, the S, the E, the ones from the pub
How many of this did you let in?
Only the Almighty can say the truth
Or when you decided to say the truth
Maybe some day you'll have the heart

Then the request came from me
The stupid one I still remained
That you should come for a week of bliss
But still you wouldn't accept this kind request
That soon you'll be back at home
But fate took control of events
You were forced back home without a plan
What a fraud you proved to be?
Why should I ever have loved you so?

I had set two tests for you
That you please call on me as planned
To say some thanks to ones that treat you right
To each of these tests you duly failed
But still my stupid brain won't take a note
To take its leave before it's hurt
The rest of the story went to script
You made all the promises in the world to me
To be my partner for the rest of our lives
To death you'll be my friend in deed
To carry the kids I've always craved

Not one of these but three you claimed
One of them will be like me
Yet again you fooled me so

But this time around that lie was real
To everywhere you followed me
Even sitting together on the train
Showing love like no one else
With the African drum playing to booth
Having climaxes day and night
The funny chair was your favourite place
You even made dinner for the very first time
Again and again you would return
And yet again I fell in love
With words of yours I made a vow
That till I die I'll be your own
That till my sleep I'll be your man

Yet again I gave my heart
This time around it was not just my heart
I gave my soul to you as well
My spirit bound to you as one
I made a request to be your man
With a ring I was intending to pledge
To vow to live my life with you
And yet again I was deceived

Why should I love you?
When without a warning you came at me
Telling me you can have all that you want
That was when he came again
That evil one of mine that is
He told you straight to go away
That you can go as you said you wished
At that point you became afraid
It wasn't time to lose your cow
That cash cow that gives you much

Then again another time
A time of dreams spent with you
A week to remember and all to hear
Making love to the middle of the night
Doing it to the sound of drums
Gbandumdum gbandumdum by the choirs of the east
The day of the sun was the crown of all
Then we parted ways to meet again
Then we planned to remain for good
To be together and forever more

Then came the arrival of those your friends
I mean the friends that have no names
I immediately knew something was wrong
I began to be afraid to meet with you
Of all your ways I have become aware
Yet again I met you up
Only to see you with those red eyes that stare
Eyes colder than the tundra of Alaska itself
Lifeless as the wilderness of Siberia
You said this time you have had enough
This perfection of mine was too much for you
This time you seem to be really sad
You hope and pray I'll forgive the wrong
Then it was that disaster struck again
I was happy at first I thought
Because at last I'll be rid of you
Then the sadness came out of the blue
Sadness that grips one as if insane
The evil one came over and over again
The little girl didn't have a chance

When our 'evil friends' returned to us
I mean the friend that was but never one
He asked to meet with you again
I said to him it was not allowed
I said to keep away from you

I tried to protect you from his evil ways
He had asked to meet with you to make a vow

It wasn't long before your secret was revealed
That yet gain you were using me
We came back from the town we'd been
And then the bitch in you returned
I was desperate for a place to live
Begged to help to find me one
We got one that needed your view
It was the fifth day as I do recall
At the eight hour to be precise
Said you were with him that caused your birth
A second time I needed your views
Scores of minutes indeed it was
But this time you couldn't be reached
All night long I tried to hear
That soft voice that came from you
But silence is all I got in return
How such a fraud you were that night
Lying that your dad is the one you're with
When in fact with a lover you had escaped
Maybe to exploit them as you do with me

But how very stupid I am indeed
Because the very next day I was back with you
This time I couldn't keep the appointed time
You said to me you were tired of me
All my pleadings were to no avail
You'd made up your mind to call it quits
Nothing in the world will make you change
That mad cold look of yours was back
The more I cried the happier you got
More wicked words streaming from your lips
Then that evil one returned to fight my course
He told you clearly the sort you were
That never at all did you give a chance

That a waster of time was what you were
He didn't even bother to say goodbye
The kiss you wanted he didn't give
Later he wrote to say you were a fake
That none could know the sort of you
Your reply was that you were so near
A woman of mine you could have been
Was it just another of your lies
Or for once you said the truth
I couldn't be convinced about how you mean
Not even you could believe yourself
Are you a fraud as they say you are?
Why wouldn't anyone fall in love with you?
When in fact you could be a cheat
You'll weave your way into any heart
Any stupid heart like this my own

I went to my friends and cried a lot
That yet again I've been used by you
That once again I have been a fool
A fool that never sees the light
They tried as most they could
To soothe my heart with words of truth
My foolish heart just would not learn
It was so resolved in its awful course
To hurt and hurt until it dies away
It soon resolved to find a way
Straight to your heart forever more
To treat you well as no one can
Much more so than you've never known
I told my friends that I had a chance
To prove to you the sort I am
To show you once that good is here
To prove to you that evil is gone
That never once will he return
I called and called but you'll not be reached
To beg you please to return to me

To give me please another chance
The chance I needed to put things right
To make it good for the two of us
To make it great so it never ends
A life of peace like we dreamed a lot
Calls upon calls I made to you
To return to me so I treat you right
When there seemed to be no hope
Then I told you I had to go
That there was one waiting in the wings
After a week you told the truth
That once again you had a man
He's had your back on the bed as others have
At least for once you told the truth
Another kind man was to suffer at your hands
He's going to be used as I have been

Tell me why I shouldn't love you
Didn't you thoroughly deceive me?
As you indeed deceived this new friend of yours
The one who gave you the D.and.G
Those cute pairs that cover the eyes
Which indeed you loved so much
A fortune to him you said they cost
Yet no qualms you felt about dumping him
Just as in fact you did to me
All those trips you went with him
All that money he spent on you
Exotic places that he went with you
North and south you drove with him
Just as sure you did with me
When the time came to hop away
All you needed was a prompt to move
Like a jet your feet was swift
To another field you went again
To pluck of all its rich rewards
This time around the field was me

It was a field you'd plundered before
This time around to complete the work
To finalise the destruction that comes from you

By now I had given up all my hopes on you
I cried a lot as if someone died
I begged and begged for you to return
Gave you deadlines and promises to be good
You had claimed that it was all my fault
Had I been patient it wouldn't have ended
Had I obliged your firm request

Let me tell why I loved you so
One of these I'll tell you now
How you took a tiny picture of me
Having known my love of art
You took your time and brought to me
A splendid portrait that I loved at once
Till now it sits on the mantle in my room
How stupid I got after this
Thinking the drawing revealed you cared
But all you cared for was for you alone
To get as much as you could from me
Use my means to care for yourself
Then laugh at me as I turned my back
What a fraud you were indeed
How exactly could I be sure of that?
Will I ever again be fooled by you?

Why shouldn't I love you?
When you deceived me so thoroughly
I will tell again how I got deceived
When you gave me a book on that tongue I loved
It looked so much like a gift of love
You said to me it was not a gift
That it was just a loan that I must repay
But you never let me return the cash

Because yet again your cold unfeeling self
With stone harsh eyes had come to play

Then it suddenly dawned on me what you were
That never my type have you ever been
I am educated and you are not
I am classy and you are not
I am exposed and you are not
I have travelled the world and you have not
I have a home and you have not
I have money and you have not
I have a job and you have not
I have a family and you have not
All you have is your broken home
Ashamed you are of your drunken dad
You never flew until I came to you
You never ate in decency until I came along
With all things I spoilt you so
Treating you like a lady when you were a whore
Now I have to stop this story of mine
Because it churns my stomach thinking of you
There's so much more that I do recall
I can't tell them in a few short words
Despite this I love you so
The pain and joy that come with you

Epilogue

Now I finish this story of mine
This is where my words will end
Although there's more I couldn't tell
The few I've said have brought me joy
Contentment of mind beyond compare
The curtain has dropped as it should have been
Now its time to take a bow
The moment for you to take your leave
Although for a fact I love you so
But I think a fraud of all you've come to be
And nothing in the world could change my mind
That a girl about town you will remain
I doubt if ever you'll change your ways
I pity the men that fall for you
I wish them luck in all their ways
I'm sure they fall for you as I have been
You'll break their heart as you did to me
Unless of course you are tamed at last
Brought to book by a lad who doesn't care a dime
But will mete to you the treatment that you truly deserve.

The park in Lower Saxony, Germany where "Why Shouldn't I Love You" was composed and written

Twinkle

Twinkle Twinkle little star
How I wonder not how you are

I know you well before we met
I dreamt a lot of you as well
I knew quite well the joy you'll bring
I felt within the betrayal that it'll lead

The pain from stabs in the centre of the back
By one you trust and called your friend

Twinkle little star
How mischievous indeed your eyes
They tell for sure what they do not mean
Like a snake green in the lush meadow
Mixing it with those you call your friends
All the while meaning no good at all

Words said only to tickle the ears
Harm to all is on your mind
Like that great Italian poet of long ago
Who cares not about who is hurt
As long as it suits the way he wants

Twinkle little star
How such a shame to have known you so

The Bitch That Thinks She's Gods

In Chelsea she was born
Others were born in *Epe* by the sea
That she'll proudly tell you
But she'll omit to let you know her true state
That she was born in Chelsea by mere accident
That in Balham in fact they lived
That even then the home wasn't theirs
They only lived as squatters there
In the home of a family they now treat with disrespect
As indeed they treat anyone that comes their way

She's got these huge massive breasts
Like those mangoes that grow in Cameroon
Kerosene I think they are called
She keeps blowing hot and cold
Like the congregation in ancient *Laodecia*
Or more like the springs of *Ikogosi*
And hot her temper boils
As hot as the month of March in *Mauduguri*

Her bottom is big and large and awry
Not round and beautiful like the Germans
Nor cute and curvaceous
Like the Hungarians and the Latvians
But droop it does as if it'll fall
She's as *bush* as the forests of *Igieduma*
She's as possessed as the priestess of *Oshogbo*
She's uncouth like the pepper sellers of *Ketu*
In fact more like the market women at *Jankara*
Or those noisy baboons on *Yankari*

She speaks softly as if she's a saint
Even the hills of *Shera* couldn't be as quiet
It seems her peace flows as the gentle spring of that beauty spot

But then she goes into the room and a turn she makes
More like the fanatics of *Kano* in all her ways
Who'll kill at will at the slightest hint of vex

Beauty she lacks extensively
Arrogance she's got abundantly
Pride is indeed her second name
Limited she is extensively
Skills she lacks comprehensively
She cannot even swim
Let alone ride a bike and…
Yet down she looks at anyone that comes her way.

Once she got into a rage
Tearing around like the wild elephants
Who roam around the rain forest of *Benin*
As usual it was unprovoked
She slammed the door at will
Shouting and screaming for all to hear
Abusing as she always seems to do
Then quickly she picked her bag
The little kid in tow
Cursing as she opened the door
Slamming the gate in your face
Not tired of what she'd done
She came right back again
A pen in hand to write
Curses that'll make you cringe
Then again the door was slammed

A second or two has passed
And there she was doing the doors
Proclaiming to them she is God's
I puzzle and wonder most times
Why my Lord doesn't slash your lips in two
With his long sharp golden sword
Exposing you as the sham that you are
A shame detracting from His great name

She has procured a dictaphone
And yet she is not a journalist
She is perusing and editing
Although she never could be an editor
All this effort for only on cause
A course of evil
A pursuit of injustice
A perpetuation of wickedness
A perpetration of crime
Perniciousness against the innocent
And yet all the ruination was performed in one name
All was done in the name of God
How you indeed besmirch His name.

It took me a while to tell this tale of mine
That bitches abound in this fair world
They could be male, female, old or young
They can't be confined to any sex at all
All they want is to take from you
What they desire is to steal your joy
They sneak their way into your heart
Telling you tales about the world around
Never for ones telling the truth about themselves
They are smooth and fine in all their ways
You'd be fooled into thinking they're real
They'll even claim they were born of God

Ask them this request for once
Once in your life time
Please change into your proper skin
That spotted skin that's peeling as well as pale
Like those of an aging crocodile in the Nile

Then it is they'll continue their tale
They'll tell you all you heard before was a lie
That you shouldn't have believed a word they said
That it was all your fault that things fell down

Then you'll respond by trying to help
Doing everything to bring peace back into your life
Giving all of the riches of your heart and more
Even your money would be all but gone
All the while you'd be thinking in your mind
That what you give should make a change
That it'll make them see how much you care
You'll speak for ever to persuade their heart
But this heart of theirs is made of flint
Melt it wont forever more

Then it was your tears and pain begin to roll
Because by now you know you're lost
You've gone into a trap without release
Who'll believe you when our face glitters like gold?
Then you give more and more to the bitch
Thinking at least they have the fear of God
Who gives his loves without reproach
What a fool you are indeed?
Because this bitch of yours could never change
They've held you in slavery and in bondage you'll remain
Unless you find a way to deliver yourself

I'll tell a tale about this bitch of mine
This same one that almost took my life
Seven times indeed I tried to kill myself
Just to escape the misery that became my own
At least be free of the torment from her
All because I fell in love
I gave my wealth, my health and almost my life

She started by crying that I was not enough
Then she nagged for me to change
To become a slave that never replies
Just like one that I grew to know
Always doing the things he's told
When these failed the abuse began

Verbal abuse of the vilest kind
None of my kin was spared her sword
Then the abuse became for real
A poke in the nose was normal for me

I had never hit anyone in my life
Then it was my bitch began to scream
All because she couldn't have her way
I must allow her to abuse my dad
Neighbours shouting for her to stop
I turned to leave to escape her rant
Then it was the door was slammed in my face
Or was it in fact the back of my head
The torrent of abuse complimenting the slam
Then it was I raised my hand
In rage at the disgrace she was bringing to us
Neighbours still shouting to shut her mouth
What a shame I brought to myself?
I felt like dying and never to return
Or at least to turn the clock back
Undoing the wrong I'd done to me

But still the bitch will not relent
When it happened again I decided to leave
To find the peace that I crave so much
I wouldn't be the monster that she called me loads
Or 'the beast' that'd become my second name

What a fool I proved to be
Because in days I was back for more
I was a victim and loved being one
I craved the abuse that was now my lot
I missed the pushing and shoving against my face
Or the jumping up and down on my head in bed
Or the evil names that I can't repeat
Hopping on my back while I try to sleep
Or making awful noises to drive me out

All of it done in the name of God
So she claims and still maintains

Why are you giving my daddy a bad name?
Why are you detracting from my father's fame?
It's fanatics like you that make Him pay
The price of his children deserting in droves
It's hypocrites like you that put people off
You lot make them turn their noses up at Him
A reputation of which he doesn't deserve
Driving away the one's who'd have had the faith

I cannot tell anymore this tale of mine
Because pain it brings from within my soul
Neither is it worth my time nor yours
Was it coming home to find the baby down?
Still having her nap for hours on end
Pew rock solid inside her pant
Lala marks all over her face
All because the bitch has had her friends
She couldn't care less if the kid died napping away
How much more of this I saw?
Even then this bitch of mine still thinks she's God's
Despite the wickedness acclaimed by all
None on earth can convince her to change
Surrounded she was by fools like her

I have a feeling I know your source
Why in fact you turned out so wickedly
It's a function of nurture and nature
Nurtured you are by a spineless dad
A man who had no balls at all
Indulged he did of you in all
Spoiling you like a rotten egg
Treating you as a special being
Condoning you in a every way
Not helped of course by that mum of yours

Uglier than any beast I know on earth
Who bore you in her peeling womb
Or should I say those scaly limbs
Carrying herself like an ostrich does
But the ancient tortoises of the Galapagos
God bless their lovely souls
Even they are more handsome than she'll ever be

You may not have cheated on me in flesh
But how many times your heart travestied?
Always philandering about what could have been
Had you hooked up with one of these
Those crumpling fanatics of whom you're so keen
For which you regretted being married to me

Very soon I say
There'll be a final call
The red rose will do its job
It'll be your end reward
A medal for all your acts
A credit for all your *doog* deeds
A message to not rest in peace
And never and ever to return
Not even in pieces
Our world would be such a better place
If and only when the likes of you are gone

Appeal

This bitch of mine
The one who thinks she's God's
A hundred times and more I called her on the phone
Each time to ask after our kids
I'm so afraid their lives will go astray
Just like those I see on the tube
But each time I get my showers of abuse
On my dad, my kin and even my mum
Despite the fact she's been dead for decades
I thought they say you never curse the dead

I think she called on me a time or two
Once to ask to sell my house
Then she called to take my toil
And finally the called to steal my wealth
Complemented of course with torrents of abuse

I'm not going to waste more time on this
She doesn't deserve this verse of ours

Now my beloved friends
Do listen to these words of mine
Losers abound around the world
This I've said and I'll repeat myself
They could be male, female, young or old
They'll creep into you like insects to plants
Then they'll eat you up from within like worms
Like soldier ants in a mound of soil
If you survive you have only the heavens to thank
Because only God above could protect you from on high

My word is for you to steer clear of these
If they come to you just take your leave
If they turn to you just run away

Should they speak to you just block your ears
Because if you don't disaster will be yours
Misery your second name
Because you're a star you'd try your best
But the more you try the more they're vexed
Count yourself lucky if you don't lose your health
Or worse still you pay with your life
Throw the bitches away and keep them there
These are my words and I hope you learn

I fell in the hole because of you
Now I lend you the wisdom I learnt
If you choose to fall despite my words
Then the fault is yours and yours alone

Book V
Those Feelings You Sometimes Have About Yourself and Everything

Ask Them

There are several people in the world
Their lives whirl around them like the wind
Ask what they do
And they cannot tell
Ask them if it's nice
And they cannot say
Request of them their purpose
And they just wouldn't know

Why on earth do they do it then?
For what reason do they exist
Why on earth are they here with us?
What on earth will they pursue?

Will they ever find the answers they want?
To all the questions that trouble their minds
Are they confused about life itself?
Are they afraid of the stuff around?

Do they ask themselves why they're here?
Do they ask a reason to live?
Do they request of themselves a leave?
A departure from the confusion that rules their minds

Why on earth do they do it?
When it never will resolve their twirl

Ask them please
How do they do it?

Why Do I Feel So Sad?

I keep asking myself this question
What has gone wrong?
Why have I got it so badly?
Why can't I do it right?
Why can't I be happy?
Why should I be so sad?

I am sad because I lost my mum
I am sad because she died so young
I am sad because I left my home
I am sad because I became a nobody
I am sad because I am educated
I am sad that it counts for nothing

I am sad because I married badly
To a lady that nearly cost me my life
To whom I lost all my toil
Even now the pain is there
A struggle to recover from what she did
The relentless abuse I suffered at her hands

I am sad because I have my kids
Who have come from below my loins
Yet to see them I cannot do,
Nor feel the freshness of their skin
Let alone touch nor cuddle them
I am sad that it damages them so
And the disaster it is doing to me
I am sad because I miss them so

I am sad because of my job
I wake up every morning feeling like I should die
I know for sure it's not what I want
I am concerned for certain that it's not my way

Yet I have to fulfil my duty everyday
Doing something that drives me nuts

It's so hard to sleep at night
Having done stuff that are meant for geeks
Seeing unsmiling faces at every turn
Who cal you nerd because you're good at work
Or bosses who'd rather you weren't around
Lame as a duck protect they won't

I am sad because of my new homeland
Where I'd come to find my peace
A place of refuge from sorrow and pain
Suddenly my consolation has tuned to isolation
That beautiful tongue that I loved so much
Has now become a reason for fear

Who on earth will rescue me so?
This broken heart that needs to mend
An honest mind that never pretends
An innocent man without deceit
A man that loves without restraint
An imperfect man with many faults
Who cares for friends and kin alike?
And would lay his life to give them one

Here come the guys with knives in hand?
Where are they heading I ask myself?
They are heading to attack the one they hate
That one who'll never be able to defend himself
To stab him everywhere with their blunt instruments

Will he die?
Will he live?
No one knows, no one can tell
Unless Divine salvation appears from up above
Assistance altruistic without needing something back

Who will rescue him from this darkness?
The darkness that has overshadowed his life
Shielding away the abundance of light
Making him see only red when there's life everywhere
Will he live?
Would he survive?
Would he be rescued?

If he does
It will be the greatest miracle of all
Then the sadness will be swept away
Like hey that burns in the summer heat

Questions

What the hell is wrong with me?
Why can't I think right?
Why can't I be happy?
Why does the world seem so grim?
Only in my head it seems
Why do I think that everyone hates me so?
When indeed no one does
When would I snap out of this melancholy of mine?
When will the dark misty clouds in my head clear
When will these ringing tones in my ears depart?

Was this not the same old me
Who was so happy a while before?
Who laughed and joked and smiled a lot
Who brought such joy to all his friends?
Who shared and gave of all he's got
Who lived and walked as if on air
Who cared but not for the perils he's had

What has caused this change in me?
What has changed my outlook on life?
Why suddenly don't I feel good again?
About me nor life itself

Why don't I realise that once there's life?
There's surely hope for one alive
Why do I feel so old when indeed I'm young?
Why do I feel deprived when I have so much?

What is this smoke in my head?
This fog in my head that's not released
Why so tight is its hold on me?
Refusing to leave despite my tries
It must be defeated and beaten for good I say
These feelings of mine won't take my life.

Now I beg to ask again
How can one be happy and yet so sad
How can you be near and yet so far?
How can you give so much love?
And yet receive so little in return
How can you ever get it right?

What is the quality of love anyway?
What is life if there is no way?
How can you ever get it right?
When it feels so wrong indeed
Where is hope when there's no faith?

How on earth can this pain go?
What on earth is one doing here?
What can be done that hasn't been tried?
What solution is there that hasn't been found?
Why does evil prevail so much?
Why do the bad seem to have their way?
Why do good lose out in the end?
Why is justice so hard to find

Tell me why and I'll give my life
Give me a reason and I'll smile like mad

The One They Love to Hate Is Here

Here comes that one
That unconventional one
So strange
So incompliant
That one who does everything his way
Never like anyone else
He's got a mind of his own
He is so creative
He loves to laugh
He loves to talk
He speaks his mind
Never holding anything back
He can be trusted
He loves all
He is so naïve

But they hate him so
Maybe because he doesn't look the part
He never learns to shut his trap
Yet admired he is indeed by most
But never of this they dare would say

Attention he pays to them
And on their knees they go at once
Weak as wick

What would they not do?
To spend their night with him
Yet day comes and they bare their teeth
Their fangs are out to claw his eyes
To hate and hate a man that's plain

Suddenly,
He passes along
And they pretend he's not there
But with the corner of their eyes
They watch his every move

What is he wearing?
What is he doing?
With whom is he talking?
Who is he speaking with?

Yet solid as a rock their face remains
Hard as flint
Without a smile
Gritting their teeth until some chip away
And yet within their rooms
In the privacy of their homes
Their mind is set to spend the night
With whom they pretend to loathe
The one they love but won't admit
To the world he's him they'd love to hate

You shouldn't be with us they say
You should be working only on your own
You cannot be in this team of ours
But look whose talking?
Who was fighting for everyone?
Who looked after all?
Who never for once thought of himself?
Who fought against the odds?
Looking ahead for the needs of all
Is it not that one they love to hate?
That geek that struggles to fit with you
The nerd that knows so much but never brags

Don't they know he cares for them?
Don't they realise he'll listen to them
Yet they hate him so
What on earth does he have to do?
Why on earth do they hate him so?

Confused!

What could I say about you?
Wahoo I said the day we met
You are simply wonderful I chant again
A beautiful blonde girl led me straight to you
She it was the path to love
A forerunner of the good to come
You were just round the corner from me

You tried so hard to catch my eye
Your green eyes looking intently for a sign
A sign of the affection I wasted so much
On others less deserving as indeed you are
Your dark brown hair groomed in the modest of ways
But then the child as dark as me
At first I thought it was a little boy
With the finest curls in the world on her
Dark and thick and lush and bloom
She in fact is from your womb
She carries your genes and looks like you
You cared for her as no one would

Then why the sudden change I spurned in me?
Why did my life turn the other way?
Why the adversity that cannot be explained?
Why did my resolution give way to confusion?
Why do I suddenly feel lost and broken?

I liked you but see what you made of me?
Now I don't even know what I want anymore
It looks to me there is only one way
One way for this doomed relationship
And that only way is disaster and rags

I should have known it from the start
In fact I did know it from the start
That all I wanted from you was friendship
But then I got myself lured away
Can't seem to find me anymore

Whenever I come close to you
I find myself getting confused by you again
My life gets shattered yet again
I feel the urge to run away
What is going on?
Wasn't it the same me that used to know everything
I have suddenly become one who knows nothing at all

How can I be happy when I don't know who I am?
What I am
Where I am
What I want to be
Where I want to be

When did all of this start?
The whole confusion began with you
It's since then I lost myself
It's since you that I lost my way
Would I ever find myself again?

Why can't you look for another man?
One who loves you and adores you so
An uncomplicated one without any qualms
Can't you see what this relationship is doing to me?
Can't you see it's almost destroyed me?
And where on earth will you be then?
When there's no man to love you so.

I used to be so happy with life in full
Now all I want to be is alone
Sometimes I feel I want to die
Will you please leave me alone in peace?
To have my calm and release for good

Can't you see I like you loads?
But then I'm sure I love you not
Can't you see I like your life
But never at all do I love your style

Can't you see I cannot make love to you?
Can't you see I cannot enjoy it?
Can't you see I am not excited by you?
Can't you see I just want you as my friend?

Can't you see I don't want to hurt you?
Can't you see I hate to see you upset?
Can't you see that I hate to see you cry?
Don't you realise it breaks me inside out?
Whenever it is I don't see your smile

Yet deep inside my heart I know
That I don't want to be your lover
I just want to be your friend
Yet you make it seem your world would end
When in fact this is not the case
You cope so well when on your own
Yet you make me feel ashamed and broken
Every time I beg you yet gain for my freedom

Can't you see I like you so
Can't you realise I don't want more
That all I want is just to be your friend
A friend in need and a friend indeed
Never your lover now and forever more

If you really love me as you claim to do
Then let me be and leave me so
Banish you do this misery of mine
And promise to be nothing but just my friend
Then the both of us can have our peace
Then this confusion will go for good.

Hello

Hello you ordinary people of the world
How very lucky you should consider yourselves
You don't have wealth
You don't have fame
You don't have all the trappings of life
Yet what you have is supreme
What you have is king

You have peace
You have hope
You have life
You have tranquillity

What on earth could be better than those?
You are richer than all of us
Because the peace you have is all we want

Sometimes

Why do I write these things?
Why do I write these verses at all?

I write them sometimes when I feel sad
Sometimes I write them when I feel lost
I write these pieces when I don't know what to do
Never do I write them when I am bored
But sometimes I write them because they ease my pain
Sometimes I write them because they make me well
Often I write this stuff when I don't know what to say
Oftentimes I write them when I am so confused

Sometimes I write them to free my mind
I often write to relieve myself
Of huge stinging pains that will heal with time
I sometimes write as a tribute to a friend
Sometimes I write to predict the unknown
Sometimes they are written to commend some deed
Sometimes to make a friend feel good

Sometimes I feel so alone
Sometimes I just wish I wasn't here
Sometimes I just wish to be left alone
Sometimes I desire to be left to breathe
Sometimes I want to have a friend
To embrace at night and never let go
Friends that remain even in the storm
Never letting go even when you tell them so

I often ask what to do with my life
I turn to the left and they don't want me there
I turn right and they hate to see my face
I smile at people and they grind their teeth at me
I laugh and their faces turn in disgust

How on earth will a man with artistic mind
Survive in this miserable old world

I wonder sometimes
Where do I really belong?
What is my lot in life?
I was in Africa and they thought I was strange
I spoke and they said my assent was white
In Europe I came and they don't like my style
I made Hungary my home and seemed happy at first
Then it was the Hungarians turned on me
The hated my face and cant wait for me to go
To Germany I went in search of peace
Then suddenly I became an anathema and a pariah

Where really is my place in life?
I sometimes write poetry of the fear I have

I check figures and yet they still complain
I should do it their way although my style is great
Where is the place for this freak of nature?
This weirdo without a habitation

I try to be good at everything
But then hardly could I call anything my own
I have friends but what really are they?
I trust none although I can be trusted by all
I keep their secrets and will do so for life
But these so called friends of mine
Without a prompt they'll tell on me

Where is the room for this sore thumb?
That sore finger that hurts like mad
But even then it demands a role
Where is the room for that clown about town?
The one who makes their noses turn as he walks by

That is why I often ask sometimes
Why is the world such a sad place?
Who on earth will change our world?
It still expects all to be the same
To think the same
Eat the same
Dance the same dull way
A world that's refusing to budge
Fixed as it is within its mould
That is why I wonder aloud about my life

Would They Ever Let Him Rest?

They will attach to him like a magnet
Hanging upon his every word
Like glue they'll remain by his side all time
Roundly showing off their pride of place

They'll suggest what really of him they want
They'll run after him on his way to work
They'll glance at him as he passes them by
They'll make comments about his everything
They'll tell how much he brings them joy
They'll suggest they'll like to have him round
Just an innocent hang about for just a while
Like a sheep indeed they'll follow him so

Meek as a lamb he'll grant their wish
Innocent like him he thinks they are
What a trap they lay in place?
As they wait their chance to get him trapped

The moment they realise he'll not oblige
To grant to them their real desire
They instantly change from saints to demons in hell

These awful parasites should just take their leave

Crazy

Who are you big head?
Are you brown or are you not?
You are pink and yet you are not
You love to talk or is that the case?
Maybe indeed you talk too much
You do indeed love to walk
Very likely you love to run

You are selfish
You are also very kind
You love your kin
But now you won't die for them

You are rash
And also very emotional
You are crazy
You are a chameleon
You can change by the second

You can bring happiness and laughter
You come with joy and peace as well
Yet sadness also follows in your track
Misery is next after every high
Broken heartedness for all your friends
Almost all at the exact same time
You switch on and off like a faulty light

You don't know what you want
Yet you do know what you need
You try so hard to please
Yet you can annoy without remorse

You are so complicated
You are so mixed up
You are mad
Yet you cannot hide how you feel

You have style
You have dress sense
You hate shabbiness
You dislike tardiness

You adore elegance
You appreciate beauty
You worship intellect
Yet not a slave to the book

You do love initiative
You appreciate originality
You love unusualness
You loathe control
You resist authority

No wonder some hate you crazy stupid s**k*r

Now Leave Me Alone

Now that you've got all the money
Now that you have all the booty
Now that the bounty belongs to you
Now that the judge has made you great
Now that you have all you want

Can I now have the peace I crave?
The peace that you cruelly denied of me
The pain that never seems to go away
Now could I have a right to life?
A gift that belongs to every man

Now may I please rebuild again
This time without the help of any man
But only of him that's up above
I hope to be wise and never again
Submit not my peace to one like you
Never again and forever more

All those liars that claim to care
But all along focused the fare from me
Especially a fee that has no end
That flows like streams from God above
Will you now leave and never return
Will you just stop your hypocritical care?
Now please leave and never return
Because this soul has found a way
To live in peace forever more
Never relying on others to have his joy

What a temper has resulted from all of this
To endure a taunt for so much time
Never reacting for the sake of peace
Then an outburst that only needs a fuse

A trigger gentle as to be unnoticed
But then an explosion beyond its cause
And never for once displays remorse

Now leave me alone
Now get the f**k out of my life
I am strange
I am wacky
I am different

But don't I deserve to live as well?
The same as you in everyway
So just go and leave me alone!

They Will Unite Wont They?

Why do they unite so well?
What is making them so close?
What is bringing them all together?
What is the centre of their debate?
What brings their minds together?
What makes them so happy?
What is the object of their joy?

Is it not their hatred of one?
Is it not their jealousy for a thing?
Is it not their objection to a personage?
Is it not their disdain for the dark?
Is it not their contempt for perfection?
Is it not the envy for what is right?

Who will save one from this snare?
A trap that lays for a time but brief
But soon will disappear without a trace
A relief we'll have at its good time

What Makes A Man Go Mad?

Is it the sight of a fair maiden?
Struggling to cope with the pressures of life
While others receive the accolades they do not deserve

Is it the constant effort to have an understanding?
Is it the frustration of being continuously denied knowledge?
By someone who is supposed to know better?
By one that should have been called a teacher

Is it the insecurity of a colleague?
A work mate that used to be your friend
But now working tirelessly to see you fail

No man could change another's destiny
The only way is up I say
To those who are ready and prepared to work

Time and Time Again

Time and time again I often wonder
Over and over again I often think
Milling over how my life should be
Thinking about where I want to be
Wondering from where my help will come
Knowing fully well that I have to survive
Realising that soon my struggles will be over
Confident that the fulfilment of my dreams is near

It may be hard for me right now
But very shortly I'll find the way
If and only if I stay true to myself
Resolving the issues that have plagued me so

Will I ever be able to take the risk?
Would I ever be able to face them down?
Telling my friends and family
That I am a man of my own
My destiny is firmly within my grasp
That I am different from the rest of them
Never conforming to the norms they set
Always probing whatever it is I'm told
Never believing until I stand convinced
Only accepting the moment I get the proof
Then alone would I put my faith
Only time will tell how this will be

'Oasis of love' in the Wilderness of the Sahara

Ancient Pine Trees in Rome, Italy. Their eyes saw a lot including the slaughtering of the apostles.

Private Park in Monastir, Tunisia.

Appreciation

My dear Readers,
I cannot conclude this piece without a few words to express my gratitude.

I wish to thank you for reading these verses and hopefully you will get to read the accompanying prose in the second volume of this book on friends which was based entirely on my life experiences.

I want to also say a big thank you to my dad Jethro Temiloluwa and the rest of my family the Ajayis and the Omogbehins namely, Biodun, Esther, Donna, Damilola, Ronke, Shola, Dupe, Bimbola, Damilola (Jnr), Doyinsola, Erik, Dayo, Kevin and Timi. Great thanks to you all for being there when all else failed.

Also, great kudos to my childhood friend Dorcas Yusuff. Many years ago this lady used her training as a solicitor to help this bereaved widow and her children whose husband had mysteriously and permanently disappeared in Abeokuta in Western Nigeria. Dokie as she is affectionately known ensured that this family was cared for financially and physically for life. Her name is now chanted like a folk song in a section of that city. She was exactly that to me at my hour of immense need, a tower of strength and support. She was a crag to run to during the most difficult of storms. She would call me, listen, advise, console, commend and reprimand when required. All in a spirit of mildness and in the kindest of ways with a sweet voice that re-assuringly says: 'I'm always going to be there for you, don't worry' and she was there all the way. What a fresh breath of air in this dog eat dog world? To this lady and her family I raise my hat any day; she is one in a million and deserves all the success that has come to her and all her own (Gani, Tomi & Dammy).

Thanks also to my ever loyal friends William Ikre (he gave up everything and took a vow to be poor and chaste for the rest of his life), Gbenga Ojo (my corner man) and also Kemi Onakoya for being there and ever loyal through these many decades.

Thanks to my boss Susan Hodgetts for being the best boss by far, the one that makes you want to come to work everyday getting in with a smile and leaving with a smile, adding value to you professionally day by day. To Riazur Rahman my assistant I say thank you for putting up with my wacky ways and being so consistently principled over many years.

To those who never changed like the weather the Montegues, The Owoeye family, The Abayomis, the D'Silvas, the Akinolas, the Adenirans (James, Lizzy, Timi & Vicky), the Ajibades and the Ogunsanyas. Not forgetting the Penson family for getting me interested in winter sports which I now enjoy very much.

Grateful thanks to my German friends and colleagues; Gerhardt Roller, Diethelm Kreter, Tanja Vince, Stefanie Strecker, Kirsten Wille, Brigitta Hulmann, Manuela Oesker, Elsa Gonzales, Crystal, Katrin Pewak and family, Stefan Hellfeier and finally Urban and Miriam Schneider. I could never forget your steadfast support at a very difficult period for all of us.

To the lovely people I met and spent time with in Hungary; Attila Der, David Townsend, Moira Vera Bansouza-Garai ('my third daughter') and the entire Garai family, the Csikora family, The Hauck family, Ljubov Gyori, Zsuzsanna Voros, Szilvia Teofilaktu, Timea Siskov, Tamas Horvath, Regina Papp, Gabor Tumele and Tamas Szanka. I thank you all for standing up when others stepped aside.

Also to those brave souls who stood up for what they believed in even at the threat of certain death, the late teenage medical objector Josie Grove has my respect forever..

...And also to the McCann family whose daughter Madeleine was cruelly snatched on the beautiful holiday resorts of Praia da Luz in the Algarve in Portugal and is still mising. Never mind the cruel scorners but I know that horrible feeling you have when you miss your children; it can be more painful than death and I understand why you've virtually given up your successful career for this course, putting your entire life on hold. May Maddie be found some day soon safe and well. Amen.

To all those in the world who have been hurt despite giving their all, who have been deprived despite loving so unselfishly and those who have been betrayed despite trusting implicitly. To you I have this assurance, good always prevails…eventually, it may take a while but just wait for it. It may be delayed but will surely come.

And finally and most importantly I would not but thank the Supreme creator of the entire universe, the father of all celestial lights, the Almighty and Everlasting God Jehovah the one with the name that is above all else, the giver of all good and perfect presents with whom there is no turning of the shadow. Had it not being for him
I couldn't be here not after eleven serious suicide attempts and still alive to tell the story following those several episodes of depression. To him alone go the praise, the honour, the glory and the adulation to time indefinite and forever.

I hope you have enjoyed these verses and hopefully I'll write some more to soothe your hearts in the future the start is a treatise on friends which will follow soon after this piece, have a great time.

Bye for now.

With love from me,

Anthony Oluwole Omogbehin

Contents